ALONG THE INSIDE PASSAGE

Stories,
Pictures and
Incredible
Facts
from Seattle
and Vancouver
to Skagway

D1534508

ALONG THE INSIDE PASSAGE

Stories,
Pictures and
Incredible
Facts
from Seattle
and Vancouver
to Skagway

by Meredith Bain Woodward
and Ron Woodward

ALTITUDE PUBLISHING

Front Cover: A Tlingit Pole looks out to Frederick Sound in Kake, AK.
Above: Johnstone Strait.
Previous page: Telephone poles and totem poles meet in Ketchikan in 1916.
Opposite: Seagulls catch a ride on an iceberg in Tracey Arm, AK. Created when chunks of glaciers break off or "calve", icebergs present only about 10 percent of their mass above water.

Library and Archives Canada Cataloguing in Publication
Woodward, Meredith Bain, 1944-
Along the Inside Passage : stories, pictures and incredible facts from Seattle and Vancouver to Skagway / Meredith Bain Woodward ; photographs by Ron Woodward.

ISBN 1-55153-218-2

1. Inside Passage--Description and travel. I. Woodward, Ron, 1944- II. Title.

FC3845.I5B34 2004   917.11'1   C2004-903050-7

Acknowledgements

The authors wish to thank contributing photographers Brian Falconer, Ian McAllister, and Michael Hayward for their generous permission to use their photo images in this project. They also wish to thank Adrienne Lindsay for her research, Ian and Karen McAllister for their assistance, Erin Falconer for her assistance and especially Brian Falconer for comments on the text.

To Myrtle, Paul and Dorothy, where it began.

Altitude Publishing Canada Ltd.
The Canadian Rockies / Victoria
Head office: 1500 Railway Avenue,
Canmore, Alberta T1W 1P6
1-800-957-6888
www.altitudepublishing.com

We acknowledge the financial support of the Government of Canada through the Book Publishing Industry Development Program (BPIDP) for our publishing activities.

Design: Stephen Hutchings
Layout/maps: Scott Manktelow
Editing and index   Elizabeth Bell

Printed in Canada by Friesen Printers

Altitude GreenTree Program
Altitude will plant two trees for every tree used in the production of this book.

Contents

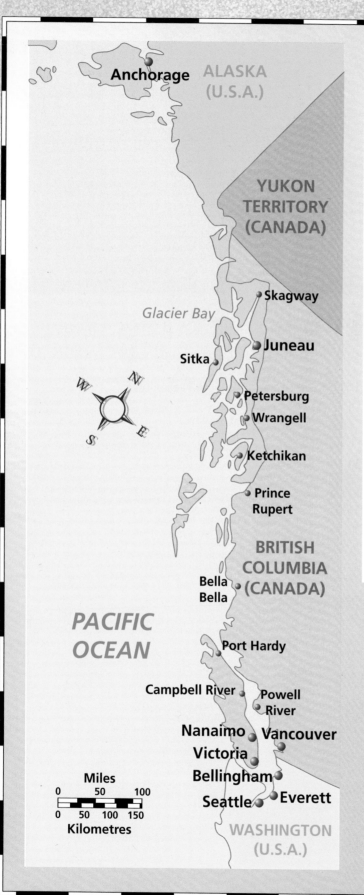

Population
(2002 figures)

Washington:
Bellingham: 69,300
Blaine: 3,770
Bremerton: 38,500
Everett: 94,400
Oak Harbour: 20,400
Seattle: 581,400

British Columbia:
Alert Bay: 546
Campbell River: 31,457
Nanaimo: 72,900
Port Hardy: 5,283
Powell River: 13,873
Prince Rupert: 16,924
Vancouver: 571,708
Victoria: 75,369

Alaska:
Haines: 1,811
Hoonah: 860
Juneau: 30,903
Kake: 710
Ketchikan: 7,922
Metlakatla: 1,375
Sitka: 8,835
Skagway: 862
Wrangell: 2,308
Petersburg: 3,224

Left: Map of the Inside Passage from Washington to Alaska.

What is the Inside Passage?

Above: *Archival image of SS Roanoke in Seattle harbour returning with gold miners from the Klondike, July 19, 1898. Prospectors discovered gold in Canada's Yukon in 1896. It took a year for word to filter back, spearheading a gold rush that attracted an estimated 100,000 men and women.*

For thousands of years, the Inside Passage has provided a 1,000-mile protected route between Puget Sound and the northern reaches of Southeast Alaska. A spectacular waterway, it crosses two international boundaries and winds its way through one of the most beautiful coastlines in the world. If you made the journey from Seattle to Skagway along the shoreline following the many bays and inlets, it would cover about 25,000 miles — the same distance as if you travelled around the globe at the equator.

Historians believe that First Nations people from Southeast Alaska canoed as far south as California centuries ago for barter and raids. European explorers and fur traders, drawing on local expertise, also took advantage of the protection of this route as they mapped, explored, and hunted, as did the miners, loggers, fishers, and settlers that followed. But it was in 1897, when the first boatload of hopefuls headed north to the Klondike gold fields from Seattle's Elliott Bay docks, that the Inside Passage gained prominence as a commercial transportation route.

Retreating glaciers of the last ice age carved the fertile lowlands, majestic inlets and craggy mountains that typify this dramatic waterway. Volcanic activity, earthquakes and glaciers are still part of the ever changing landscape. The many species of flora and fauna that exist along the Inside Passage all have a story to tell that documents this sometimes harsh evolution, from the blue ice of slow moving glaciers to the careful sniff of a foraging grizzly and the majestic soaring of a bald eagle.

With both untamed wilderness and cosmopolitan cities along its route, a journey today through the Inside Passage has the traveller visiting some of the world's most beautiful cities, experiencing unique aboriginal cultures, viewing wildlife in spectacular natural habitat, and enjoying some of the most exquisite scenery on the planet.

There are thousands of islands, bays, and inlets along the Inside Passage; it would take a lifetime to explore them all. "We've been sailing up here for ten years," says one veteran visitor to the area, "and every time it's a new experience. Even when you go back to the same place, it's different. You never see the same thing twice."

Concerned about disruption and destruction of habitats, in recent years some voices have been giving a different twist to that sentiment. You'll never see the same thing twice, they argue, because many species will soon become extinct. They see much of the Inside Passage as a valuable and unique ecosystem that needs protection against development and exploitation if it is to retain the wildlife, forests, ocean quality and marine life that draws hundreds of thousands of visitors every year. ∎

Left: A Kwakwaka'wakw thunderbird pole in Alert Bay, BC.
Top right: Detail of a weathered pole in Haines. AK.
Bottom right: A big house in Haines, AK.
Opposite: Totems at Comox, a coastal community on Vancouver Island, in the 1890s. The name is abbreviated from "Komuckway", meaning "abundance" or "riches" referring to the abundance of berries and game.

Totem Poles

Northwest Coast First Nations culture fascinates people all over the world, with totem poles one of the most well known artifacts. These carvings can be found throughout the Inside Passage, from to Haines and Skagway.

Although totem poles are universally recognized as belonging to Native culture, only six Nations traditionally created totem poles: Haida, Nuxalk, Kwakwaka'wakw, Tlingit, Tsimshian, and Coast Salish.

Totems are a traditional way of telling the stories of families and clans as well as keeping records of important events. The stories will be about a myth, legend or a person. A traditional pole will also contain a family crest. The most common crests are eagle, raven, thunderbird, bear, beaver, wolf, killer whale and frog. It is not possible to understand the story a pole tells just by examining its elements. The poles are more like guides that aid in interpretation.

There are several types of traditional poles, including interior house posts (Kwakwaka'wakw and Haida), doorway and house poles (Haida and Kwakwaka'wakw), mortuary poles (Haida, Tlingit, and Tsimshian), and memorial poles (Haida, Tlingit, Kwakwaka'wakw and Tsimshian). Coast Salish poles tended not to be free-standing and were often high relief carvings on walls of ceremonial dance houses, on beam support posts, or grave figures.

Carvers traditionally created totems from western red cedar, which was plentiful, tall, straight-grained, and resistant to decay. Although most only last 60 to 80 years, some surviving poles are 200 years old.

Totem pole carving flourished with the development of the sea otter fur trade both because chiefs commissioned more poles to indicate wealth and status, and because trade with the Europeans resulted in tools for speedier production. But as contact with Europeans increased, First Nations cultures faltered and the art of carving waned after 1870. Fortunately, a new generation of carvers emerged in the mid-twentieth century and the art is currently alive and flourishing. At least two communities on the Inside Passage, Alert Bay, BC, and Kake, Alaska, claim the tallest totem pole in the world.

UBC's Museum of Anthropology, Vancouver, has one of the most impressive collections of traditional poles and carvings in the world. Other museums and parks along the Inside Passage also have good collections. But the lucky traveller who comes across a decaying moss-covered pole laying in the brush of an uninhabited village will have the opportunity to experience the power of these awesome pieces firsthand. ■

Inside Passage Facts

Mile O: Seattle, Washington — N47°35′ W122°21′

Northernmost city: Skagway, Alaska — N59°27′ W135°19′

Total distance: 1050 nautical miles

Distance in Washington: 125 nautical miles

Distance in BC: 575 nautical miles

Distance in Alaska: 350 nautical miles

Distance along coastline: 40,225 km (25,000 miles)

International boundaries: 2

Major European explorers: Juan Francisco de la Bodega y Quadra, George Vancouver, Vitus Bering

Tallest mountains:
Mount Fairweather (BC-Alaska border in Glacier Park) 4663 m (15,298 feet)
Mount Rainier (southeast of Seattle) 4392 m (14409 feet)
Mount Waddington (north east of Knight Inlet) 4019 m (13,185 feet)

Major river systems: Fraser, Skeena, Stikine

Distances
(in Nautical Miles):

Seattle to:
Victoria: 72
Vancouver: 129
Campbell River: 228
Port Hardy: 336
Bella Bella :433
Prince Rupert: 613
Ketchikan: 659
Wrangell: 749
Petersburg: 771
Glacier Bay: 945
Juneau: 879
Haines: 950
Skagway: 962

Top Left: Deep fjords, carved by retreating glaciers, mark much of the Inside Passage. This steep mountain-side is part of Cousins Inlet in the Great Bear Rainforest section of BC's coast.
Bottom left: Near Ocean Falls on BC's coast, Cousins Inlet, is typical of deep fjords found along the Inside Passage.
Right: Dramatic mountain peaks of the Coast Range overlook much of the Inside Passage. This is one of the twin-peaked "Lions", a familiar landmark near Vancouver.

Natural History

Shaped over the last several million years as a result of shifting tectonic plates, erupting volcanoes, glaciation and weather, the contours of the Inside Passage continue to develop and change today. There are three main geographic areas running lengthwise: the Coast Mountains of the mainland, the "Coastal Trough" of the Inside Passage itself, and the Insular Mountains (of Vancouver Island, the Queen Charlotte Islands, and the Alexander Archipelago). The Insular Mountains were at one time a low-lying mountain range, but they were flooded as the ice cap melted at the end of the last ice age.

Although the last phase of the last ice age, the Wisconsin Glaciation, melted into oblivion about 10,000 years ago from most of North America, massive glaciers and permanent ice fields still cover a significant portion of the land bordering the waterways of the Inside Passage. Evidence of the retreat is easily seen, from the massive-house sized boulder it deposited just outside Coupeville on Whidbey Island, Washington, to the large bowl-shaped cirques hollowed out of the mountains lining Lynn Canal, Alaska.

The Coast Mountains, which developed about 20 million years ago, dominate the landscape from south to north. Although various waves of glaciation have shaped them, initially they were formed by the collision of tectonic plates beneath the earth's surface — rigid sections that float on the hot liquid core of the earth, 10 to 30 kilometres thick.

Besides creating mountains and reciprocal depressions, the collision also left behind several potentially active volcanoes, part of the "Ring of Fire" that extends around the entire Pacific Rim. (One such volcano, Mount St. Helen's, in southern Washington, erupted very dramatically as recently as 1980.) Remains of lava flows and volcanic cones are evident at various locations along the coast.

The constant tension between the Pacific Plate and the North American Plate along this line also causes the earthquakes that have had, and will continue to have, a dramatic impact on the land and its people. The Alaska Earthquake of 1964 (which centered in Anchorage, not Southeast Alaska where the Inside Passage travels) is the second largest ever recorded. While such a massive occurrence is rare, Alaska experiences an average of 10 low-register earthquakes a day, a reminder of the constant activity under the earth's surface. (This hotbed of seismic action has one delightful legacy — the many hot springs that dot the coves and inlets of the Inside Passage, providing a welcome relief to ancient as well as modern-day mariners.)

As everywhere else on planet earth, climate and

topography are intricately interrelated, each influencing the other. Although it is a relatively long area, generally the Inside Passage has a mild, wet, marine climate influenced by the warm Pacific Ocean and its prevailing westerly winds.

Much of it can be classified as temperate rain forest: mountains and ocean in close proximity, mild temperatures, substantial rainfall. But it hosts a variety of micro-climates and terrain, from the low lying, relatively dry conditions of the Gulf and San Juan islands to the icy peaks in Glacier Bay. The variations in Southeast Alaska alone, for example, range from an average of 391 cm (154 inches) of annual precipitation in Ketchikan to only 66 cm (26 inches) in Skagway.

As you would expect, the sea dominates daily life along the Inside Passage. Twice a day the tides ebb and flood (a diurnal system) and throughout human history, the people who live along the ocean shores have been tied to these rhythms. In some areas, where the water flows through narrow openings of land, currents reach speeds of up to 16 knots, among the fastest in the world. Mariners must be constantly vigilant; those who aren't suffer dire consequences.

The area supports a variety of flora and fauna that reflects the marine and rainforest environment. Dense forest tracts sustain a wide range of wildlife, among them deer, wolves, moose and the legendary grizzly and kermode bears. The marine life is also legendary, with visitors flocking to experience everything from tide pools to breaching whales.

Travelers, marvelling at the seemingly endless expanse of wilderness and the occasional sighting of a dolphin or grizzly, are often unaware that all is not as it seems. Environmental advocates have been concerned about the health of the ecosystems in this area in recent years, citing issues such as

Left: Sunset at St. John's Harbor, Sumner Strait, AK
Right: Gulls nest on rocks scraped bare by retreating glaciers in Glacier Bay, Alaska, where over 240 species of birds have been identified.

diminished salmon stocks and grizzly habitat and threats to old growth forests. Those with economic interests view the area in a different light. Logging companies, mining operations and fish farms see the area as a wealth of economic opportunity. It is a great challenge facing the stewards of the area, which ultimately, is all of us. ∎

Cetaceans

Whales, dolphins and porpoises belong to the Cetacea order of marine mammals. There are about 80 species in the world today. The most commonly seen whales on the Inside Passage are humpback, minke, and gray. The dolphins and porpoises most commonly seen are Pacific White Sided dolphins, harbor porpoise, Dall's porpoise, and orca (or killer) whales. (While they are called whales, orcas are actually the world's largest dolphin.)

Cetaceans are mammals, not fish. They breathe air through their lungs; they are warm blooded and must maintain a body temperature of 35° to 37°C (95° to 99°F); and they give birth to live young and have mammary glands.

Left: *Gregarious Pacific white-sided dolphins (Lagenorhynchus obliquidens) are very acrobatic and love to ride the bow waves of boats. Commonly seen throughout the Inside Passage, they travel in schools that can number several hundred, sometimes with other dolphin species. They manoeuvre and find food using a system of echolocation.*

Right: *The endangered humpback whale, similar in size to a large passenger bus, is the most commonly seen whale in Southeast Alaska. Most humpbacks make yearly migrations between warm winter waters in the south for breeding and cold summer waters in the north for feeding.*

Opposite left: *Black bears (Ursus americanus), which actually can be brown, cinnamon, creamy white or even blue-grey, are plentiful along the Inside Passage. These are omnivorous creatures, eating whatever is available, but relying heavily on salmon. Males can weigh up to 300 kg (661 lbs).*

Opposite right: *Noted for its large bulbous proboscis, the Northern Elephant seal (Mirounga angustirostris) can sometimes be seen in BC coastal waters, but usually not further north on the Inside Passage. The largest known Elephant weighs about 2722 kg (6000 lbs) and is about 5.5 m (18 ft) long, but average size is a mere 600 kg (1323 lbs) and 3.6 m (12 ft). The deepest divers in the ocean, they have been known to plunge to depths over 1524 m (5000 ft). They also migrate further than any mammal, sometimes traveling over 9600 km (6000 mi).*

They can be divided into two categories: those with teeth (odontocetes) and those that use plates of baleen to feed (mysticetes). Orcas, for example, have teeth, while Gray whales use baleen for food gathering. The diet of cetaceans varies, depending on location, season, and whether they have teeth or not. Baleen species use the plates as a filtering system, feeding on small fish and plankton. Those with teeth tend to be more predatory, feeding on fish, squid, and marine mammals. Migration patterns of cetaceans are closely linked to their search for food. Most coastal First Nations hunted whales during the northern migration, some more intensely than others, but whales play a prominent cultural role in all Northwest Nations. The Haida, Tlingit and Kwakwaka'wakw traditions are among those that celebrate and honour relationships with the whale. Whale motifs are common on totems, baskets and traditional clothing. One commonly held belief was that a village of whales lived on the ocean floor. If so inclined, a whale could drag an entire canoe load of people down to the village. Once there, they would become transformed as whales. In one account of Haida tradition, whales who washed up on beaches were people who had drowned and wanted to communicate with those still living.

The European whaling industry, now outlawed, began in the 1830s and lasted in the Pacific Northwest until the 1960s. Historic use of whales by Europeans included: oil (for lights, margarine, cold cream); baleen (for corset stays, umbrella ribs, brushes, brooms, carriage springs); skin (for handbags, shoes); bones and teeth (for jewelry, piano keys, fertilizer); as well as meat for human consumption.

Today, whale watching is one of the most popular recreational activities for visitors to the Inside Passage.

Commonly Seen Wildlife

(* Endangered or Threatened)

Marine Mammals
Cetaceans (see pg. 11)*
Harbour seal
Otter (sea* and river)
Sea lion (California and Stellar's*)

Land Mammals
Bear: Black and Grizzly
Deer
Moose
Mountain goat
Porcupine
Raccoon
Squirrel
Weasel family (weasel, mink,
    marten, wolverine)
Wolf (Gray)*

Land Birds
Eagle
Crow and raven
Osprey
Peregrine falcon
Woodpecker

Shorebirds and Waterfowl
Auklet
Black oyster-catcher
Cormorant
Ducks (Barrow's, Common
    Goldeneye, Harlequin)
Geese (Canada, Snow)
Gulls (Glaucous-winged, herring,
    Bonaparte, Ring-Billed)
Heron
Kingfisher
Loon
Murrelet*
Pigeon Guillemot
Puffin
Sandhill Crane
Sandpiper
Scoter
Sooty Shearwater
Storm Petrel
Tern
Western Grebe

Underwater Life
Anemone
Barnacle
Clam
Coral
Crab (Dungeness, Rock, King)
Herring
Jellyfish
Kelp
Mussels
Octopus
Oysters
Prawns
Salmon*
Scallops
Sea Urchins
Seastars
Sponges

Above: A Tlingit village on Gastineau Channel near Juneau ca 1885.

Theoretically, whales can be seen at almost any spot along the route, but popular viewing locations include Lime Kiln State Park on San Juan Island in Washington, Johnstone Strait in BC, and Sumner Strait, Icy Strait, Glacier Bay and Frederick Sound in Alaska. ■

Human History

Experts believe that humans have existed at various places along the Inside Passage for thousands of years. They don't however, agree on how the first humans got there. One widely accepted theory suggests that human beings arrived ten to 12,000 years ago, utilizing the land bridge across the Bering sea, and dispersing to unglaciated areas. As the glaciers retreated, descendents of these hardy nomadic souls found their way to the lush Pacific Coast.

Another theory postulates that when the ice sheets began retreating 14,000 to 16,000 years ago from the Gulf Alaska and the BC coast, small areas of land were gradually exposed — and that some areas were actually ice free. Vegetation quickly took hold, providing pockets for seafaring people to settle. A major archeological find at Prince of Wales Island in Alaska in the 1990s was among several recent discoveries up and down the Pacific Coast of North America that supports this idea. The theory opens the door to the possibility that the first people did not come from Siberia over a land bridge, but travelled by boat from other land areas of the Pacific Ocean.

For the time being the debate goes on, but we do know that human beings were in the area 10,000 to 12,000 years ago. While discoveries of basic tools provide evidence of this, it took several thousand years for the land to stabilize and reliably support the people. Although First Nations oral history puts it much earlier, archeological excavations suggest a systemized culture developed about 3000 to 4000 years ago, in any case, one that reflected a deep involvement in the elements of the natural world around them.

Because the resources on land and sea were so abundant, these early residents did not have to travel great distances for survival, as did other aboriginal cultures. With accessible marine life such as whale, halibut, salmon and shellfish in the ocean, and trees plentiful on the land, they could take care of basic needs like food, shelter, and clothing without being nomadic (although they often moved seasonally). The great cedar trees, for example, provided strong, yet soft, wood for houses, canoes, clothing and baskets. With the means of basic survival close at hand, the people developed a rich culture of art, legend and storytelling that celebrated a close spiritual relationship with the world around them. Decoration of utilitarian items like house poles, baskets, and clothing reflected this culture. Surplus food and goods became trading currency both with Interior Nations and coastal neighbours.

Major language groups along the Inside Passage are Tlingit, Tsimshian, Haida, Wakashan (Haisla, Heiltsuk, Kwakwaka'wakw), and Coast Salish. A complex social

structure existed within each First Nation group, usually based on genealogy. Although each Nation shared many elements of life in common, they also were very different from one another: Haida were distinct from Coast Salish, for example, and Tlingit from Kwakwaka'wakw (Wakashan). Villages often attacked one another for revenge or retrieval of property or to take slaves. (These conflicts extended to Europeans when they began trading in and settling the area, but no major battles have been recorded as with the Plains people.)

Beginning in the mid-16th century, several European nations, driven by a desire for expanded trade routes and power, developed an insatiable curiosity about the world along the northwest coast of North America. Russia, Spain, England and later America, were eager to avail themselves of the area's natural riches, first with the development of a fur trade, and later in the exploitation of resource-based industries like mining, fishing, and forestry.

Place names along the Inside Passage reflect all of these nationalities from the Strait of Juan de Fuca (a Greek sailing for Spain) to the city of Prince Rupert (British royalty) and Baranof Island (a Russian administrator).

The negative impact of European contact on First Nations cultures that had flourished for centuries is well documented. The Haida, for example, dropped from an estimated population of 14,000 to 20,000 to around 800. Disease, alcohol, and the introduction of elements like guns and non-traditional tools either directly decimated numbers or derailed traditional ways of doing things. Many First Nations of the Inside Passage were assigned to reservations that exist today, and Native land claims are a major political issue in British Columbia. (Only one reservation exists in Alaska.)

Above: *Coastal Natives depended on the cedar tree for everything from housing to clothing. This Nakoatok (Kwakwaka'wakw) chief's daughter is wearing a robe woven from cedar bark. During a potlatch, the chief's eldest daughter was symbolically enthroned on the heads of her slaves.*

Obviously, the topography of the land has had an enormous influence on human settlement. The highest density of population is along the southern Inside Passage in the Georgia Basin. Vancouver and Seattle are large metropolitan areas sprawling over gently rolling lands between mountains and sea. Vancouver Island, with its relatively gentle terrain, particularly in the southern and eastern portions, also supports a relatively high population density. Further up the coast, as the terrain becomes more rugged, population centers drop dramatically. The population of the entire state of Alaska, for example, is 627,932, while Seattle and Vancouver each have populations just shy of that (537,150 and 571,708, respectively).

The Inside Passage played an important role in the developing economies of the lands it embraced. Just a few weeks after Captain George Vancouver sailed up Dean Channel near the Native settlement of Bella Coola in 1793, Alexander Mackenzie completed his historic overland journey from Montreal to the Pacific Ocean, in search of more fur trade routes. The Russians, British, and Americans all participated in an aggressive fur trade along the Inside Passage, which almost wiped out the sea otter population.

Although the rugged terrain has prohibited the Inside Passage from becoming heavily populated, many small communities sprang up beginning in the mid-19th century. Discoveries of rich inland ore deposits, like in BC's Cariboo region in 1858, spurred the development of other resource-based industries like forestry and fishing and soon canneries, packing plants, lumber operations and pulp and paper mills began to appear. As the population and industries grew, railroads were built, opening up the coastal areas around Seattle, Vancouver, and Prince Rupert even more. Immigrants from China, India and Europe were among those that worked in the plants and mills attached to these industries. The development of floating communities was common, with complete towns including stores and schools, moving from place to place along the Inside Passage as economics dictated. Vessels busily steamed up and down the coast transporting goods and people.

But by the mid-20th century, coastal resource-based economies of logging, fishing and mining began to falter and many communities with them. Although urban centres like Vancouver and Seattle continue to grow, the coastal culture is not as vibrant as it once was — countless towns and villages have completely disappeared in the last few decades. Evidence of the glory days of resource-based communities can be seen in many spots along the Inside Passage in deserted towns, abandoned machinery left in the forests, or skeletons of boat hulls along the shore.

With First Nations people moving toward self-government and environmental issues gaining increasing prominence, the choices and patterns of human settlement are creating a new legacy. Some communities are finding new life providing services to a growing tourism industry that embraces everything from sport fishing and whale watching to hotels and restaurants. ■

Above: *Native settlement on Burrard Inlet, ca 1868. Today Burrard Inlet is Vancouver's harbour and a major seaport. The surrounding land is among the most expensive real estate in North America.*

≈Who Came Second?

No one disputes that the First Nations people were the first residents along the Northwest Pacific Coast. Archeological evidence confirms human presence at the end of the last ice age, about 10,000 years ago. But who was second?

Most history books say Spanish, Russian, American and British explorers were next, around the middle of the last millennium. But some researchers suggest that the second wave of humans to set foot on the northwest coast of North America were not from Europe, but from Asia. And that they were here as early as 485 AD.

No hard archaeological evidence exists of such a trip, but a Chinese history written around 585 AD describes the journey of several Buddhist monks who travelled to a land across the Pacific. Some scholars think this was British Columbia. And some First Nations myths and legends mention strangers who visited before the Europeans, adding credibility to the theory. It is possible that the monks then headed south to Central America, which would explain Buddhist and Hindu elements found in Mayan art from the same time period.

The fact that the Chinese were excellent mariners (they invented the rudder and the compass) added to the existence of the strong west-to-east flowing Pacific Ocean currents, makes some historians believe they have a very strong case. Some say it is inevitable that fisherman from China or Japan would be blown off course, and end up on the coast of North America. Archeologists have found some artifacts at First Nations sites that could be evidence of Asian contact, but no one can say for sure when the contact occurred. So for now, history buffs are left with a big tantalizing question. ■

Petroglyphs

Hunting and gathering cultures the world over have practised the art of rock carving for centuries. Known as petroglyphs, these collections of stylized symbols and signs chiseled into rock are found all along the Inside Passage.

Although some of the Inside Passage's petroglyphs could date back 10,000 years, archeologists don't know exactly how old the carvings are or even what they mean. But they are often found at the water's edge — above or below high water marks. Sometimes they appear to depict dangers to marine navigation or important natural events, like a good salmon run. Other carvings may commemorate births, deaths and potlatch celebrations. Some complex designs are believed to record legends and histories. Circles, spirals, "O", and "Y" designs are the most universal. Experts think that shamans may have created

Above: A petroglyph on the beach at Wrangell, AK.

some petroglyphs in ceremonies honouring the spirits in order to bring good luck to their people.

One of the easiest places to view petroglyphs along the Inside Passage is at Wrangell's Petroglyph Beach, a state historic site. Some 40 rock carvings litter the shore at the site, which some archeologists believe could date back 8000 years. Near Nanaimo, BC's Petroglyph Provincial Park also provides accessible viewing. Although viewing these ancient and mysterious carvings in a designated area is an extraordinary experience, nothing beats stumbling across a rock carving, on your own, on some desolate beach. Some other places where petroglyphs can be observed are the Gulf Islands, Port Neville and Mackenzie Rock.

Time Line

8,000 BC - Glaciers melt and humans leave microblades and cores at campsites, suggesting Siberian migration.

500 AD - Possible Asian contact.

1579 - Sir Francis Drake reaches the Pacific Northwest coast in search of the Northwest Passage. Historians aren't sure if he actually sailed into Juan de Fuca Strait.

1592 - According to an account published in 1625, the Greek sailor Juan de Fuca reaches the coast of the Pacific Northwest between 47° and 48° North latitude, sailing into the strait that later bears his name. Some historians claim it didn't happen.

1741 - Vitus Bering, a Dane by birth, charts the coast of Alaska for Russia in one of the largest expeditions the world had seen, looking for the Northeast Passage. Fur trade with First Nations people begins.

1742 - Russians file the first scientific report on the North Pacific fur seal.

1774 - Juan Perez of Spain, exploring as far north as the Queen Charlotte Islands (Haida Gwaii) and Prince of Wales Island, is the first European to describe the Pacific Northwest coastline, although he did not sail in the Inside Passage.

1775 - Bruno de Hezeta y Dudagoitia claims the Pacific Northwest for Spain. Juan Francisco de la Bodega y Quadra, also under the Spanish flag, sails north as far as Sitka, Alaska.

1778 - Captain James Cook maps the Pacific Northwest for Britain, eventually reaching Bering Strait, but he did not explore the Inside Passage.

1789 - George Washington is elected first president of the US.

1792-3 - Captain George Vancouver tries to find the Northwest Passage and charts the Pacific Coast to Southeast Alaska.

1793 - British fur trader Alexander Mackenzie completes the first overland journey of North America from Montreal to Dean Channel near Bella Coola.

1792 - Catherine II of Russia grants a monopoly of furs in Alaska to Grigorii Shelikov.

1799 - Alexander Baranof establishes a Russian post at Sitka.

1805 - Americans Meriwether Lewis and William Clark complete their overland journey from St. Louis to the Columbia River.

1805 - Russia ships its first cargo of furs from Alaska to China.

1843 - The Hudson's Bay Company establishes a fort at Victoria on Vancouver Island.

1846 - A treaty between the US and Britain establishes an international boundary at the 49th parallel.

1851 - The first settlers arrive at the site of present day Seattle.

1853 - President Polk creates Washington Territory.

1858 - Prospectors discover gold in BC's Cariboo region, a key factor in the settlement of the province.

1867 - US Secretary of State William Seward's purchase of Alaska from the Russians for two cents an acre becomes known as "Seward's Folly". The fur seal population, stabilized by the Russians, begins a rapid decline.

1871 - BC becomes Canada's fifth province.

1874 - George Halt allegedly becomes the first white man to cross the Chilkoot Pass looking for gold.

1877 - US troops withdraw from Alaska.

1878 - Sitka and Klawock open the first canneries in Alaska.

1879 - John Muir visits Glacier Bay

1800 - Gold is discovered in the "Juneau Gold Belt".

1883 - The Northern Pacific Railroad links Tacoma with the east.

1885 - The Canadian Pacific Railway is completed.

1889 - Washington becomes the 42nd state of the US.

1896 - Klondike Gold Rush begins, lasting for just three years.

1924 - Alaska gets its first airmail delivery.

1942 - Japan occupies the Aleutian Islands.

1954 - Boeing's 707, the first jet transport, makes its inaugural flight.

1958 - US President Eisenhower signs the Alaska statehood bill.

1959 - Tlingit and Haida win land claims suit in Alaska.

1964 - An earthquake centered in Anchorage is felt throughout Southeast Alaska.

1975 - Seattle native Bill Gates creates Microsoft.

1975 - Large cruise ship companies promote "Inside Passage" route to Alaska.

1980 - Mount St. Helen's erupts.

1995 - BC fishermen attack an Alaska ferry in Prince Rupert over frustration with joint US-Canada fishery talks.

1998 - The Nisga'a Indians of BC sign an agreement with the BC and Canadian governments over land, resources and self-government.

Naqapenkim

"Ten Times a Chief"

Born in 1880 a member of the Kwakwaka'wakw Nation, Mungo Martin was destined to become a major force in the survival of Pacific Northwest First Nations cultural traditions.

The story is told that when just a baby, his mother took him to a great carver, Yakutglasomi, asking him to assure her son's future as an artist. The great man made a paint brush from four of baby Mungo's eyelashes and some porcupine bristles, which he then used when painting designs.

At a ceremony a few months later, his mother put her baby inside a drum. His father gently beat on the outside, crooning songs to him about his history and culture. As he grew older Martin listened attentively to the songs and stories that had been handed down from generation to generation and learned carving traditions from his stepfather, Charlie James.

A major means of passing along the stories and dances that made up the ceremonial life of the Native culture was destroyed with the prohibition of the potlatch. But Mungo Martin remembered, reportedly recalling over 400 songs and stories, including those from Haida, Tsimshian and even far away Navajo nations.

As a young adult, with Native people unable to survive by following traditional ways, Martin became a commercial fisherman. But the skills that had been engrained in him early on were not lost. One day, for example, when he broke a propeller, he was able to carve a new one out of a piece of driftwood and be ready to go on the next tide. During the potlatch ban, Martin continued to carve poles and masks and participate in secret potlatches.

In the late 1940s he was asked to help restore some totem poles at the University of BC in Vancouver,

Above: *Celebrated Kwakwaka'wakw carver Mungo Martin helped retrieve an entire Nation's culture by instructing a new generation in the art of pole carving and other traditions. Here he works with his son, David Martin, in the 1950s.*

among them a pole he had carved in Alert Bay in 1902. In 1951 when he was in his seventies, Mungo Martin was invited to Victoria to become the resident carver at Thunderbird Park, where he set about restoring old poles and carving new ones. When the potlatch ban was lifted in 1952, Martin and his helpers built a replica of the native house of his birth at Victoria's Thunderbird Park to celebrate the event. His last great potlatch was held on December 15, 1953.

Credited with teaching many of today's finest carvers, Mungo Martin crafted his last totem in 1961. The 37-foot pole was commissioned by the Canadian government and sent to Mexico as a goodwill gesture. He died in August 1962 leaving behind a rich and immeasurable legacy.

Above: A halibut design decorates a Tlingit house in Saxman, near Ketchikan, ca. 1909.

Economy

Although the Inside Passage includes two US states and one Canadian province—different political systems, different histories, different values—the people who make a living outside the big cities have much in common. Trees, fish, minerals and the waterway itself have been largely responsible for the settlement and development that have occurred up and down the coast since the arrival of the European fur traders.

The mountains of the Inside Passage are heavily mineralized. The discovery of coal in places like Bellingham and Nanaimo helped settlement and stimulated development, but it was the big gold rushes of Barkerville in BC (1858), Juneau (1880) and the Klondike in the Yukon (1897) that had thousands flocking along the Inside Passage, triggering transportation and logging, as well as agriculture.

The larger cities, like Seattle, Vancouver, and Victoria and even Juneau, have developed diversified economies based on industries such as transportation, government, manufacturing, and education. Seattle, for example, is home to mega-corporations like Microsoft and Boeing. (And let us not forget Starbucks.) But for decades, small coastal communities have relied almost exclusively on the fish and the trees to make a living—a reliance that continues, albeit tentatively, today. ■

First Nations Pronunciation

Haida: hy-dah
Kwakwaka'wakw: kwk-wak-ya-wak
Salish: say-lish
Tlingit: kling-kit
Tsimshian: sim-she-an

≈Fishing

Commercial fishing in the Inside Passage dates back to the fur trade era of the early 19th century, when the Hudson Bay Company began buying salmon from First Nations people to feed its employees. The industry expanded dramatically when the first salmon canneries opened: in BC on the Fraser River in 1867, in Mukilteo, Washington in 1877, and in Klawock in Southeast Alaska in 1878.

Halibut

(Hippoglossus stenolepsis)

The largest marine flatfish found on the Inside Passage, halibut can weigh up to 225 kg (500 pounds), grow to 3 m (9 ft) long, and live 60 years. They live at depths from 18 to 2000 m (60 to 3600 ft), spawning in winter in the deep water. A 65 kg (140-pound) female halibut can spawn about 2.5 million eggs.

Mature adults migrate over a range of 3200 km (2000 mi) in an area extending from California to the Bering Sea and Japan. Bottom feeders, they eat crab, clams, squid and a variety of fish. They have well developed teeth on both sides of their jaws and two eyes on top of their "heads".

Halibut played an important part in First Nations art, particularly in Haida culture. Myths and legends tell of Raven stealing octopus bait from halibut hooks. First Nations people used to carve hooks for catching halibut from bone: the best traditional hooks can bring in fish up to 23 kg (50 pounds).

Tlingit legend says that when a fisherman's wife cast aside a small halibut on the beach, the fish began thrashing about with such violence that it eventually caused the land to split, creating the Queen Charlotte Islands.

Above: *Fish packers cleaning halibut in Prince Rupert, 1957.*

Above: Fishermen at work aboard a commercial halibut ship in 1914.

Major operations were centered around the three main river systems of the Inside Passage: the Fraser (Steveston and Vancouver, BC), the Skeena (Prince Rupert, BC), and the Stikine (Petersburg, AK); with many smaller operations flourishing up and down the coast. In 1901, 70 canneries processed fish between the Fraser River and the Portland Canal on BC's coast. In the 1920s, Prince of Wales Island hosted 25. Ketchikan had 13 canneries in 1940. Although the fishery has diminished dramatically in recent years and many coastal communities have suffered, harvesting from the sea continues to be important — for species that include salmon, halibut, crab, prawns, oysters, clams and herring.

Fishing is currently the number-one private sector employer in Alaska, providing more jobs than oil, gas, timber and tourism. More than 4.7 billion pounds of fish and shellfish were harvested in 2001, with a value of $US871 million. (This is down from 1991, when the total harvest was 5 billion pounds, worth over $US5 billion.)

Fish farming, introduced in the 1970s, is a controversial part of the Inside Passage fishery. Banned in Alaska in 1989, fish farming is blamed by many for the decline of the commercial fishery; they say fish-farming practices contaminate local stocks and waters and may lead to the total destruction of local species. In BC and Washington, fish farms produce salmon, trout, and shellfish. ∎

≈Forestry

The forest industry experienced a similar cycle historically, of almost frantic activity, that has taken a downturn in recent years. While early shipbuilding demanded lumber and spars, the mining boom from the 1850s to the 1900s created an increased need for lumber and mills, and the completion of three trans-continental railway systems (at Prince Rupert, Seattle, and Vancouver) created expanded markets.

In BC, the Hudson's Bay Company built the area's first mill in 1848 at Millstream, near Victoria. Andrew Pope and William Talbot began milling logs at Port Gamble, Washington in 1853, using their own timber, their own ships, and their own lumberyards to create one of the first integrated lumber operations, still in operation today. Arriving in Everett, Washington in 1900, to expand his Minnesota lumber company, Frederick Weyerhaeuser joined the game: his forestry business grew to be the largest in the world. In Alaska, the forestry industry took a little longer to develop due to the high costs of labour and transportation. The first sawmill appeared south of Wrangell in 1879, providing lumber for the cannery boom, but it was many years before forestry became a major industry.

Five major commercial species are logged along the Inside Passage: Sitka spruce, red and yellow cedar, Douglas fir, and western hemlock. The largest stands of Sitka spruce in the world are found in BC and Alaska.

As with fishing, forestry continues to be important to communities on the Inside Passage, but the downturn in the industry has had serious implications for many. Thorne Bay, off Southeast Alaska's Chatham Strait, for example, the largest logging camp in the United States in the 1980s has no logging

Fred Athorp
Halibut Fisherman, Ketchikan

"Sometimes I get awful tired of the fishing," Ketchikan fisherman Fred Athorp admits. "But it's a lifestyle that I like." Athorp used to be a dairy farmer before he decided to try Alaska for the summer in 1959. He never left. He's been fishing on his own vessel full-time since 1972, long-lining for halibut and black cod and trolling for salmon.

Long-lining involves setting ground lines — about six miles of it for black cod, with hooks every six feet in about a half mile of depth; bigger hooks for halibut, set about 18 feet apart. "We usually set two strings," says Athorp. "We anchor it out, go back and pick it up, haul it up, take the fish off, rebait it, and set it again." He fishes with his wife when he's trolling for salmon, with his sons when they're after halibut and cod. Hard work.

But he likes the fishing culture. "My boat's paid for," he says. "We don't drive as hard as people who've got big payments to make. We go up and down the coast about 500 miles. My wife and I enjoy each other's company. And we visit; we know somebody in all the places we go."

But there are downsides. Since 1923, the halibut fishery has been regulated by the International Pacific Halibut Commission. He's given an individual halibut quota and it's strictly enforced. "Last year I went 200 pounds over and it cost me about $5000," says Athorp. "One fish." Fishers calculate the weight of their catch by using a scale that shows length and average weight. "My two sons were very careful, but they were heavy fish. We're allowed 10 percent over, but if you go one pound over that, they fine you and take all the fish over your quota, including the ten percent. And then they take it away the next year.

Above: *Fred Athorp takes the time between fishery openings to keep the* Cheryll A *looking trim.*

One fish. Oh boy."

And one fish, if it's a halibut, can be huge. The biggest one he remembers catching was eight feet long and weighed 500 pounds. They'd shot it, but still had trouble getting it aboard. (Halibut fishers often carry a twenty-two for the big ones. "They'll break your leg," says Athorp. "They're much easier to get in if they're dead.")

The weather can be a bit tricky at times, too. "We're about 30 miles offshore and it's pretty nasty sometimes. Mean seas — waves close together and steep, coming from three directions, no relief." He picks his weather windows these days, but when he had a crew to pay he tended to push it more. He's been out in winds of up to 100 knots (64 knots is considered hurricane force), but the worst weather he recalls was 70-knot winds and 25-foot seas. No Loran C in those days. An old radar that only showed clutter in the wild waves. After several tense hours, he made it safely into an anchorage, but only because he was familiar enough with the area to tell where he was by depth readings.

He doesn't drive that hard anymore. "We're usually anchored up by six o'clock in the evening," he says. "Some people will come in to sell, unload, get some groceries, ice up and be gone. We come in, we sell, we go tie up and go take showers, and the next day we'll do our laundry and get our groceries, and if the weather's nice the next day we'll leave."

He sees a similarity between fishing and farming. "It's the harvesting thing," he says. "You work a lot of hours when you have to, but then you have a lot of time off." He chuckles. "I'm kind of semi-retired."

Does he plan to be fully retired any time soon? "Well, a friend of mine — he's not going to fish anymore," Althorp reports. "And he's 97. I don't know if I'll be at it that long." But for now, he's taking advantage of a sunny Ketchikan day to put a final coat of varnish on the bright work before he heads out with his wife for some trolling. And visiting. And enjoying life in his adopted state of Alaska.

Above: Horse loggers skid trees on Denman Island in BC's Gulf Islands in the early 1900s.
Right: The rugged landscape along the Inside Passage made settlement and exploration a challenge. These men are portaging a boat near BC's Dean Channel in 1906.
Opposite: Although logging companies still occasionally use floating camps along the Inside Passage, they were the norm in the early part of the twentieth century. This outfit is in BC's Port Neville off Johnstone Strait in 1927.

activity at all today. And here, as elsewhere, there is a continuing debate between conservationists and forestry companies and managers about the future of Inside Passage forests. ■

≈Tourism

Despite the downturn in forestry, fishing and mining, the natural resources of the Inside Passage are fuelling a new economy for the 21st Century: tourism and recreation. Cruise ships have been taking tourists through the Inside Passage since John Muir wrote about the area in the 1880s; large-scale tourism gained a foothold in the last part of the 20th century.

The Alaska cruise ship industry began a rapid growth in the mid-1970s, providing a blast of economic fresh air to the communities of the Inside Passage. A 1999 study estimated that cruise ship passengers and crew spent about $181 million annually in Southeast Alaska. The industry brings hundreds of thousands of people through the Inside Passage each year, the majority departing from Vancouver or Seattle. Most of the large ships don't stop until they get to Alaska, which doesn't help the ailing fishing and logging communities in between, but the larger industry appears to have spawned a number of small tourism, eco-tourism and recreation companies. Small boutique cruises, fishing lodges, wildlife-viewing ventures, First Nations tours, eco-adventures, helicopter sightseeing, and a host of other businesses appear to be giving the people of the Inside Passage a chance to find new ways to make a living from the natural resources. ■

Inside Passage
Cruise Ship Facts

Length of Alaska cruise ship season: 22 weeks
Total number of sailings from Seattle (2002): 79
Total number of sailings from Vancouver (2002):
   331
Estimated revenue for Seattle businesses (2002):
   $USD42.5 million
Estimated revenue for Vancouver businesses (2002):
   $508 million
Total number of passengers visiting Juneau in 2001:
   683,077
Total number of crew visiting Juneau in 2001:
   293,176
Total number of arrivals in Juneau in 2001: 539
**Most number of cruise ships visiting Juneau in one
   day in 2001:** 7
Largest cruise ship to visit Juneau (2002):
   Royal Caribbean's Vision of the Seas (2400-
   passenger capacity)
Number of stops it made in Juneau (2002): 17

**Consumed by the 2200 passengers on Celebrity
   Cruise Line's Infinity in one week in May 2001:**
Eggs: 110,820
Vegetables: 25,736 pounds
Beef: 24,236 pounds
Chicken: 20,311 pounds
Fish: 13,851 pounds
Beer: 10,100 bottles
Wine: 3,400 bottles
Milk: 3,3260 gallons
Coffee: 2,458 pounds
Lobster: 2,100 pounds
Cookies: 1,936 pounds
Ice cream: 600 gallons
Champagne: 200 bottles

Brian Falconer,
Eco-tour Operator and Tourism Consultant, Duncan BC

The double-masted schooner bobs energetically against the outside dock at the Prince Rupert Yacht Club. The wind is blowing strong on this day in early June and the vessel's white hull and varnished timber bowsprit and masts are impressive against the blue sky. "Ninety-two feet," says the bearded man on the dock beside her when asked about the vessel's length. "And almost a hundred years old," he adds. It makes you think of riding along on fresh sea breezes, of new lands, adventure.

That's just what it's supposed to do. The bearded man is Brian Falconer, the vessel the *SV Maple Leaf.* Until recently, Falconer was the owner and captain of this eye-catcher and as such, operator of one of the oldest ecotourism businesses on the Inside Passage.

Originally a luxury sailing vessel built in 1904 for a wealthy Vancouver, BC lumberman, the *Maple Leaf* was seized by the federal government during WWI, various parts destined for munitions. After the war, it was recommissioned for halibut fishing in Alaska. One of the Canadian government's first "buyback" boats, Falconer found her in 1980, docked up the Fraser River, patiently waiting for the next chapter in her life.

Falconer has worked on the coast for a long time, not always as its friend, but developing, in spite of himself, a deep abiding love of the place. He started as a forest company bush pilot, then built a Rivers Inlet fly-in sportfishing lodge, which he

Above: *Brian Falconer (right) and* SV Maple Leaf's *new owner Kevin Smith in Prince Rupert harbour.*

followed up by converting a WWII sub chaser and running a charter business. Now he's a respected ecotourism advocate and environmentalist. He says the *Maple Leaf* was a large part of the shift. "The places that we've sailed, the places that she's taken me, have shaped me," he says. "It is who I am. The last 20-odd years have utterly changed me.

"The more you know about the coast, the more you respect it really deeply, the more you understand it," he says. "And I guess that's what's made me more involved in trying to help protect it." He has become an active member of the Raincoast Conservation Society, involved in the preservation of the Great Bear Rainforest.

He has also been deeply influenced by working with First Nations people. He's worked closely with elders and hereditary chiefs in setting up his programs. "From the elders and hereditary chiefs you just get a whole outlook on life that's really rich and very, very valuable."

Falconer and his ex-wife spent six years restoring *SV Maple Leaf* before launching Maple Leaf Adventures in 1987. Today, the company offers a dozen tours to different Inside Passage and Queen Charlotte Islands (Haida Gwaii) destinations from May to October. "People are really affected by what they see," he says. "Because we're small, the line between guest and crew is quickly blurred. We're just a bunch of new friends travelling together. We'll have a nice meal and a glass of wine and part of the conversation is 'What did you see? What did you learn?'"

For some *Maple Leaf* clients, exploring the Inside Passage has turned out to be a life-changing experience. One couple, Falconer says, recently invested a half a million dollars in a large tract of land on BC's Sunshine Coast to maintain it for wildlife.

When the *Maple Leaf* leaves the dock to cross Dixon Entrance and head north in the morning, it will be Falconer's last trip. But you get the feeling that he's not done with the Inside Passage. "For most people in the world," he says, "this is very exotic. How many places can you see a black bear, a kermode bear, a bunch of killer whales, a humpback and a couple of wolves on the same day? I've spent 17 years sailing up the coast here and there are still hundreds — thousands — of places that I haven't been."

Top: *Mungo Martin presents a ceremonial copper crest to Elizabeth, the Queen Mother, in London in 1958. With him is his adopted granddaughter, Helen Hunt, herself a chief three times over.*

Bottom left: *Kayaking is popular all along the Inside Passage. These vessels await the next day's adventures on the shores of Parker Island in BC's Gulf Islands.*
Bottom right: *Passengers on an SV Maple Leaf eco-tour enjoy a unique way to experience dolphins.*

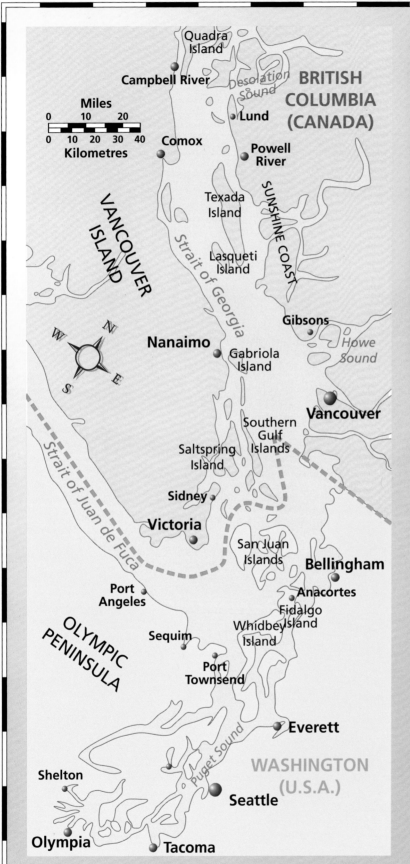

Quadra Island

Campbell River

Desolation Sound

BRITISH COLUMBIA (CANADA)

Miles
0   10   20
0 10 20 30 40
Kilometres

Lund

Comox

Powell River

Texada Island

SUNSHINE COAST

VANCOUVER ISLAND

Strait of Georgia

Lasqueti Island

Gibsons

Howe Sound

Nanaimo

Gabriola Island

N
W   E
S

Vancouver

Southern Gulf Islands

Saltspring Island

Sidney

Strait of Juan de Fuca

Victoria

San Juan Islands

Bellingham

Port Angeles

Anacortes

Fidalgo Island

Sequim

Whidbey Island

OLYMPIC PENINSULA

Port Townsend

Everett

Shelton

Puget Sound

WASHINGTON (U.S.A.)

Seattle

Olympia

Tacoma

Above: The open gateway of the Peace arch, which marks the US-Canada border at Blaine WA, stands as a symbol of peaceful relations between the two countries. The 20.4-metre monument was dedicated in 1921; the grounds have been a provincial park since 1939.
Left: Map illustrating the Inside Passage from Seattle to Campbell River.

THE GEORGIA BASIN: PUGET SOUND TO DISCOVERY PASSAGE

Above: The Strait of Georgia, which runs from the San Juan Islands north to Desolation Sound, dominates the Georgia Basin. This section is just north of Vancouver looking from Howe Sound across to Vancouver Island.

The first leg of the journey north through the Inside Passage is through the Georgia Basin, a 280-nautical mile-long inland waterway that reaches from the southern end of Puget Sound in Washington State to the northern end of Bute Inlet in British Columbia. The Georgia Basin's major bodies of water are the Strait of Juan de Fuca, which runs east-west to the Pacific Ocean, and the Strait of Georgia, which runs north-south, dividing the mainlands of BC and Washington from Vancouver Island. In addition to the mainland coast, the area also includes Washington's San Juan Islands, as well as BC's Gulf Islands and south to central Vancouver Island.

The Georgia Basin is part of an area known to past and present First Nations as the Salish Sea. This traditional waterway of the Coast Salish people extends from Puget Sound as far as Johnstone Strait, which borders northern Vancouver Island.

The Georgia Basin has by far the highest population density of any area along the Inside Passage, with the vast majority of people living in the metropolitan areas of Seattle, Victoria, and Vancouver. Human settlement is almost continuous from Olympia to Sechelt on the mainland and, to a lesser degree, from Victoria to Campbell River on Vancouver Island. And it makes sense that this should be so, with the relatively flat lands of the islands and mainland providing a hospitable environment for settlement, agriculture, transportation, and industry.

The predominant First Nations people in this area are the Coast Salish. Unlike other coastal First Nations people, the Salish carving traditions did not include totem poles, nor was the potlatch a ceremony practised by most groups. (Salish knitting and weaving that use hand spun wools and natural dyes are highly prized today). Evidence of First Nations settlements and camps can be found throughout this area and First Nations motifs are commonly seen.

Some describe the coastal region as one big river estuary, dominated by the Fraser River system in BC. Rich farm lands, a result of retreating glaciers and silt deposits from rivers, extend over much of the area. A great deal of this fertile soil has been relinquished to the housing demands of a growing population around the three major population centres, but farming is still important, producing everything from alpacas and hazelnuts to milk cows and potatoes in both Washington state and southern BC.

The mountains on both sides of the Georgia Basin belong to the Coast Range. In the southern part, the Cascade Mountains dominate the mainland. Mount Baker, east of Bellingham, and Mount Rainier, southeast of Seattle, are two volcanic peaks that provide majestic backdrops to southern

Top left: Port Townsend, on the northeast tip of the Olympic Peninsula, is a Washington State Ferries terminus connecting with Whidbey Island.
Top right: A cruise ship heads out of Seattle's Elliott Bay enroute to Alaska. Prominent on the skyline is the landmark Space Needle, built as part of the 1962 Seattle World's Fair.
Right: A modern metal-sculpture totem pole overlooks Semiahmnoo Bay at Blaine, WA.
Opposite: Seattle's first European settlers landed at Alki Point (in West Seattle) in 1851.

Georgia Strait and Puget Sound. In the northern part, the flat to gently rolling land gives way gradually to steep sided inlets and rocky shores on the mainland.

Most of this portion of the Inside Passage is sheltered from the Pacific Ocean by BC's Vancouver Island. At 31,284 sq km (12,079 sq mi), it is the largest island on the Pacific Coast of North America (but only tenth largest in Canada). Victoria, BC's capital city, is on its southern end; it began as a strategically-placed Hudson's Bay Company fort built in 1843.

As well as being the starting point for most Inside Passage cruises to Alaska, the Georgia Basin is popular with recreational boaters today. The Puget Sound area near Seattle, the San Juan and Gulf islands, the Sunshine Coast, Jervis Inlet and Desolation Sound are legendary cruising grounds. ■

Cascadia

Although the lower part of the Inside Passage can be divided up along political lines into the entities of Washington and British Columbia, it is seen by some as part of Cascadia, a 400-mile corridor with eight million residents, stretching from Eugene, Oregon to Vancouver, BC. With a regional economic output of $250 billion annually, if it was a country, it would be the tenth largest economy in the world.

This is, no doubt, largely due to the presence in the Seattle area of Boeing, the largest aircraft manufacturer in the world, Microsoft, the largest personal software company in the world, and Weyerhaeuser, the largest lumber company in the world.

Since the 1970s, several organizations, mostly business- or environmentally-based, a few tongue-in-cheek, have promoted liaisons on a number of issues and activities. They argue that geography is more important than politics and that the area is a distinct cultural and economic unit.

Cascadia is also a term used by geologists to describe the chain of volcanic mountains that runs from northern California to the north end of Vancouver Island. It is influenced by the Juan de Fuca Plate, which, as it moves beneath the continent, causes earthquakes and volcanic activity. ■

Philip Raisor,

Lock Operator, Sequim

Philip Raisor is always happy to chat with visitors to Seattle's Chittenden Locks. But his attention remains on the steady flow of vessels heading through the system, in or out of Lake Washington and on to Puget Sound. "Every locking is different," he says on a sunny September evening. "You've got different sized boats, different mentality, different knowledge, different skills."

Guiding a boat into a single lock and safely out the other side requires focus and attention from everyone involved. "My biggest problem," says Raisor, "especially in the large lock, is when folks don't tie their lines properly. If I don't cut one a week," he says with the flicker of a smile, "I feel neglected. We work just as hard as we can, but you've got to be one step ahead at all times."

Philip Raisor is an 18-year veteran on the job. It was not the Kentucky native's boyhood dream to work on shipping locks, but he's glad he ended up here. He points out a couple of kingfishers dive bombing each other over the lock. "They do this every night," he says, chuckling. "It's real entertainment."

It's also deadly serious business. Raisor recalls one incident several years ago when one vessel's crew tied

Above: Philip Raisor at the Chittenden Locks.

a line up and didn't release it when the water was going down in the lock. The cleat pulled out of the deck and hit a crew member on the head, fatally injuring him. "You've got to be on top of it all the time," he repeats.

On a good three-day weekend, the attendants will assist 3,000 vessels through the locks. Peak times are the summer months, when recreational boaters are more active, but in the spring and fall the Alaska fishing fleet also keeps them busy.

The annual Seattle Seafair festival is a real challenge. "It's the funniest day," says the US Army veteran. "This year, on Saturday afternoon we put 122 boats in here. And most of them don't know if they're coming

or going because they've been partying all week." He laughs. "I've been mooned and flashed with the best of them."

Boaters aren't always as ready as they can be, even though the facility offers classes in procedures. "It's a big problem — people not being prepared," he says. "You tell them ahead of time you want them port or starboard, but then they'll come in without their fenders down or their lines ready. They don't understand the concept of the water going up and down."

Soon to retire, Raisor takes a moment to contemplate what he's learned in his years on the job. "Let's put it this way, I like to treat a person like he treats me," he says in his relaxed twang. "You do that and the whole world's a lot better off." But he's not retired yet, and as a large mahogany classic cabin cruiser eases up the small lock, Raisor quickly moves forward to the vessel, back to the task at hand. "You get more with honey than you do with vinegar!" he calls back over his shoulder with a grin. And then he's all business, giving final instructions, guiding one more boat safely through the Chittenden Locks.

Puget Sound

Strictly speaking, Puget Sound is an estuary, a semi-enclosed glacial fjord mixing the salt water of the Pacific Ocean with freshwater from the surrounding watershed. Named in 1792 for Lieutenant Peter Puget of the Vancouver expedition, who explored its south end, this body of water stretches 145 km (90 mi) from Juan de Fuca Strait to Olympia. It's a busy deep water seaway (240 m/787 ft maximum depth), used heavily by freighters, fishers, and other commercial vessels and popular with whales, dolphins and recreational sailors — despite winds that can gain speeds of 50 to 60 knots.

The eastern side of Puget Sound is highly urbanized corridor stretching from the state capitol of Olympia in the south to industrial Everett in the north, with Seattle at its centre. In sharp contrast, the west side of the sound is bounded by the gently rolling landscape of the Kitsap Peninsula with the mountains of the Olympic Peninsula standing sentinel behind. Many people who work in the Seattle area commute from Bainbridge Island, Vashon Island and the peninsula via ferry. It's a picturesque, historic area, with a slower pace and many small towns nestled in its coves and valleys. The Olympic Mountains provide a spectacular backdrop to these communities; some of its peaks reach 2440 m (8000 ft) only 40 km (25 mi) from sea level.

The Puget Sound area supports a population of 3,275,847 and covers roughly 16,000 sq km (6300 sq mi). Native Americans are Coast Salish and include the Suquamish, S'Klallam, Chemakum, Skokomish and Toanhooch. ■

The Port of Seattle

Ranking in size as a US container port: 6th
World ranking as a container port: 40
Annual value of products transported through Seattle's docks: $USD36 billion
Number of steamship lines regularly serving the port: 26
Number of major transcontinental railroads serving the port: 2
Number of trucking companies serving the port: 100
Area: 450 acres of container-handling space
Number of container cranes: 25
Products handled include: chilled fruit, vegetables, forest products, automobiles, steel, cruise ships and grain.
Other facilities owned by The Port of Seattle: Seattle-Tacoma International Airport; Fishermen's Terminal and Marine Industrial Center; Shilshole Bay Marina; Bell Street Pier

≈Seattle

Although Puget Sound extends south past Seattle to Tacoma (site of the Sea-Tac International Airport) and Olympia (Washington's state capital), many consider Seattle "Mile O" of the Inside Passage. Small numbers of cruise ships began sailing this route in the 1880s, but it was from Elliott Bay's docks that thousands of hopefuls headed north to the Klondike in 1897.

"The nearest opposite shore of the main inlet ... the lofty pine trees, which appear to compose one uninterrupted forest between us and the snowy range ... the serenity of the climate, the innumerable pleasing landscapes, and the abundant fertility that unassisted nature puts forth, require only to be enriched by the industry of man with villages, mansions, cottages and other buildings to render it the most lovely country that can be imagined." So wrote British explorer Captain George Vancouver in May of 1792 as he gazed upon the forested land that we now know as Seattle.

Young compared to most large North American cities, Seattle got its start when a group of 24 adults and children landed at Alki Point on November 13, 1851. The following year, after enduring a rough winter on the point, several people made land claims on the eastern shore of Elliott Bay, at what is now downtown Seattle. These founding fathers — A.A. Denny, W.N. Bell, C.D. Boren, D.S. Maynard, and Henry L. Yesler — gave their names to many of the modern city's major streets and roads. By 1880 Yesler had a thriving sawmill operation and the foundation of a lumber economy that remains today.

The natives referred to the place as Tzee-tzee-lal-itch, ("little portage" because of a trail to Lake Washington. But the early settlers chose to name their fledgling city after Chief Seattle of the Suquamish people. Although the Chief had given early traders and explorers a bit of a rough time, he was acknowledged as a good friend by the early pioneers, and they honoured his passing with a monument at his burial site (located across Puget Sound at Suquamish in Port Madison Bay.)

Rumours of a transcontinental railway hookup brought a population and land boom to Seattle in the 1890s. The railway terminus materialized, Seattle flourished, and today it is a major metropolis in the Pacific Northwest, hosting major corporations such as Microsoft, Boeing, and Weyerhaeuser. The birthplace of the Starbucks coffee empire and home to music legends Jimi Hendrix and Kurt Cobain, the "Emerald City" also provides an excellent base for outdoor recreation enthusiasts.

Ferries and bridges are a way of life for Seattle residents. With Lake Washington on one side and Puget Sound on the other, you're never very far from water. ■

The Islands

The islands of the Georgia Basin have been attracting people since human habitation began in this area. With the waters of Puget Sound and the straits of Juan de Fuca and Georgia lapping their shores, they include the islands of Puget Sound and the San Juan archipelago (the San Juans in the US and BC's Gulf Islands), as well as the much larger Vancouver Island.

Petroglyphs, middens and other evidence of First Nations settlements, some of which date back about 5000 years, can be found throughout these areas. European settlers found the rich soils, mild climate and gentle landscape appealing and homesteading started as early as the 1850s. The smaller islands also became popular for retreats and summer cottages. Island life continues to be a West Coast attraction from Puget Sound's Vashon and Bainbridge islands to Quadra and Cortez at the northern end of Georgia Strait.

Vancouver Island, which makes up the western shore of most of this section of the Inside Passage and the next, is considerably larger than either the San Juan or Gulf islands. The largest island on the Pacific Coast of North America, it covers an area of 31,284 sq km and reaches 460 km from the Strait of Juan de Fuca north to Queen Charlotte Sound. Victoria, BC's capitol is at the southern tip of the island. Logging, mining, fishing, tourism and farming are also important contributors to the economy. ■

Left: Orcas Island's Moran State Park is the largest in Washington, and it contains the highest point in the San Juans, Mt. Constitution. If you drive all the way to the 734 m (2407 ft) summit on a clear day, you get a 360-degree view that includes Vancouver BC, Victoria BC, and Seattle.
Right: The north end of Whidbey is separated from Fidalgo Island by Deception Pass. Officials estimate that 3.5 million people stop here annually to marvel at the impressive steel cantilever-truss, 55.5 m (182 ft) above the water, built in 1935 by the American Civilian Conservation Corps. There are actually two bridges here; one is 158 m (511 ft) and the other is 298 m (976 ft) long. It cost more to paint them in 1983 than it did to build them in 1935.

Washington

State Capital: Olympia
Population: 5,685,300
Area: 172,447 sq km (66,582 sq mi)
Motto: Alki ("By and by" — Salish)
Nickname: Evergreen state
Flower: Coast rhododendron
Gem: Petrified wood
Tree: Western hemlock

33

Elain Genser,
"The Kite Lady",
Victoria, BC

If you tell Elain Genser to go fly a kite, she'll do it — happily. And literally. She calls herself the "Kite Lady."

Currently a resident of Victoria, Genser has flown kites up and down the coast and around the world since she first happened upon the sport at Victoria's Clover Point in 1982. "I thought it looked neat," she says. "Pretty soon I was buying kites like mad." Now she designs and makes her own, gaily coloured pieces that range from abstract mosaics to Canadian Mounties.

On a sunny fall afternoon in September 2002, she sits behind a roped off area in the middle of a large field at Whidbey Island's historic Camp Casey; she's the "featured flier" at the annual Whidbey Island Kite Festival. She keeps her eye on the dozen or so of her distinctive kites that are currently up in the air, making sure the wind keeps them aloft, fine tuning when necessary.

Being part of a tradition that was first documented over 2000 years ago was an eye opener for Genser. "I was introduced to a whole subculture that I never knew existed," she says. "There are clubs, magazines, websites, and festivals — kiting events are held all over the world!" Her laughter contains a trace of astonishment, as if surprised by her good fortune.

There's a camaraderie that exists between kite makers. Several stop by Genser's station as we chat. She interrupts our conversation to confer with Kevin, a colleague from Australia, about the day's events. "The mass ascension is scheduled for 12:30," she says, "but I don't know where it is!" Kevin will find out. He

Above: Elain Genser, framed by her kite creations.

heads off toward the official tent at one end of the field.

The mass ascension is actually an earth-bound event, held every day at kite festivals: participants parade across the fly area with kites of specified designs. However, kite flying is not without it's ethereal side. "It can be very spiritual," Genser admits. "The wind — you can't control the wind. The kite is on a line and you have some control about what goes up there, but the wind is going to blow it wherever it wants to go. And if the wind stops, the kite's going to fall." She hands me the string of the one she's planning to show in the mass ascension — a mosaic creation outlined in black, with dozens of brightly coloured squares. The line tugs and dances. There are forces at work here: physics, meteorology, matters of the mind.

During the summer, enthusiasts organize festivals up and down the Pacific North West Coast — "Vancouver, White Rock, Whidbey Island, Ocean Shores, Pacific Beach,

Comox, Sechelt. You can go to one every week, if you want," says Genser. But she has also flown kites in such exotic locations as Tasmania, Mongolia, and Bolivia. She's even flown a kite over the equator on a tall ship.

She's been to festivals that are a week long, with 30,000 kites in the sky. "It's a huge gallery," she says. "And believe you me, when all those kites come down, that sky looks dull." She's had shows of her kites in art galleries, but she prefers the sky. "At home in Victoria," she explains, "when there are no distractions, I'll go down to the field and I'll put up five or six kites on a nice day. Then I'll sit in my chair and assess what they look like, and maybe I'll change a tail or I'll take one kite down and switch it up with another. It's like painting the sky."

The Juan de Fuca breeze has died momentarily and Genser rushes out onto the field to rescue a downed Mountie, her "signature kite." She expertly teases and tugs the line, getting it aloft once again. Then she hurries back and plucks up a mosaic kite. "I paint the sky, that's what it's about," she says as she hurries off to the mass ascension. "It's a connection, a wind thing."

≈Whidbey Island

The eastern shores of Admiralty Inlet lap against Whidbey Island, which claims it is the longest island in the lower 48 states — 72 km (45 mi) from top to bottom. And wherever you are on the island, you will never be more than five miles from shore. With only 59 cm (20 in) of rain annually, the climate is good for flying — everything from kites to airplanes. It's also out of the way of commercial flight paths and has little electrical interference, which is why the US Navy has a base at Oak Harbour. Built in 1941, the base houses 7500 employees responsible for EA-6B carrier-based jets and A-6 Intruder attack bombers.

Joseph Whidbey, master of Captain Vancouver's flagship Discovery, explored the island in 1792. Early inhabitants were the Salishan, followed by European settlers in the 1850s, attracted by the lush fertile land left by the retreating glaciers. ■

≈Victoria

Three million tourists can't be wrong. That's how many visitors flock to this city of 73,500 people every year. In summer, the downtown streets are lined with colourful flower baskets and a variety of horse drawn buggies and vintage cars compete with double-decker buses to ferry the folks around. They come to see the legendary Empress Hotel, the world-famous Butchart Gardens, and for the "olde-England" ambience.

But it's not just tourists who come here. The largest city on

Above: Victoria's Inner Harbour is the site of BC's parliament buildings as well as the historic Fairmont Empress Hotel.

the Strait of Juan de Fuca, Victoria is British Columbia's provincial capitol; the historic Parliament Buildings are the focus of many politicians, bureaucrats and lobbyists.

Located on the southern tip of Vancouver Island, Victoria began in 1843 as a Hudson's Bay Company fur trading fort, and was incorporated as a city in 1862. Named for Britain's Queen Victoria, who ascended the throne in 1837, the city has been the provincial capitol since 1868. For many years it was the busiest seaport north of San Francisco, a result of its protected Inner Harbour. (A walk along Foul Bay Road near Beacon Hill Park on a stormy day will show what it needs protection from. The wind and waves from the Pacific Ocean can be wild.)

With the demise of maritime industries like sealing and the completion of the transcontinental railroad in 1885, Vancouver became the more dominant economic force in the province, but Victoria remains the political centre.

The actual city is quite small in area, but the Capital Regional District extends the population to 305,287 including the farming region of the Saanich Peninsula as well as the Canadian naval base at Esquimalt. The nearby city of Sidney is the terminus of the BC Ferry connection to the mainland.

The area is also known as a haven for retirees who are attracted by its mild climate, slower paced lifestyle, genteel architecture, and terrific scenery. ■

Above: Built in 1843, the Hudson's Bay Company's Fort Victoria replaced Fort Vancouver on the Columbia River when Oregon Territory became part of the US in 1846. This photo was taken in 1860.

≈San Juan Islands

Although there are 172 islands in the San Juan group, most are not habitable, and the Washington State ferries stops at just four. All these islands with their inlets, estuaries, hills and valleys were formed by retreating glaciers thousands of years ago, but they have provided a haven for everyone from farmers and smugglers to artists and sailors.

Seattle mayor and millionaire shipbuilder Robert Moran was 49 when he decided to retire to the San Juans in 1907 after doctors gave him only a few months to live. Moran, who built a 54-room mansion, Rosario (now a popular resort) where he entertained the likes of Teddy Roosevelt, credited the mild climate, natural beauty, and relaxing atmosphere with restoring his health: he died in 1943 at age 86. His donation of 6000 acres of land resulted in Moran State Park on Orcas Island.

The biggest island, San Juan, was named for the Viceroy of New Spain by Spanish explorers in 1791. The British arrived a year later. The Pig War notwithstanding, settlement of the islands was sporadic, although by the mid-1870s Orcas orchardists were producing prize-winning fruit. The real growth began in the 1950s when retirees "discovered" the San Juans. Now the islands are a very popular "getaway" for residents on both sides of the border. ■

≈Gulf Islands

Depending on the tides, there are over 200 islands in BC's Gulf Islands, ranging from tiny Mitlenatch and tropical Savary islands in the north part of the Georgia Basin to Discovery Island in Juan de Fuca Strait just north of the US border. Once part of Vancouver Island, they were separated from that larger land mass and the mainland by glacier action.

The largest in this group is Texada Island about half way up the Georgia Basin. Other major islands are Saltspring, Gabriola, Galiano, Mayne, Pender, Saturna, Hornby, Denman, Thetis, and Lasqueti. Known for their attractive Mediterranean climate, eight of the islands are regularly served by BC Ferries.

Archeologists have identified the first inhabitants as Coast Salish who settled the area about 5500 years ago, although First Nations history suggests they had lived in the area much longer. Middens, petroglyphs, pictographs and other indications of these early settlements can be seen throughout the area.

The Gulf Islands are part of the Nanaimo Sedimentary Basin, a shallow coastal marine trough formed about 70 million years ago. But creatures have been living here for longer than that. Paleontologists have identified marine reptile fossils and dinosaur fragments near Courtenay on Vancouver Island. Some rocks found on Saltspring Island have been dated at 370 million years old.

The Gulf Islands were explored by the Spanish and English in 1791 and 1792. Earliest European settlers were David and William Hogan who farmed on Gabriola Island as early as 1854. Other early settlers included Kanaka sailors from Hawaii and freed African-American slaves.

≈

The Canadian government is in the process of creating a new national park with land donated and purchased on several of the southern Gulf Islands. ∎

Strait of Georgia

Named by Captain George Vancouver after British King George III, Georgia strait supports seven pulp and/or paper mills (Campbell River, Crofton, Nanaimo, Powell River, New Westminster, Woodfibre and Port Mellon); six deep water ports (Vancouver/Roberts Bank, Fraser River, Campbell River, Powell River, Nanaimo and Squamish) and 30 marine parks and ecological reserves.

It is a busy thoroughfare, stretching about 140 nautical miles from the San Juan Islands in the south to Campbell River in the north and ranging from 20 to 40 km (12 to 24 ft) wide. Tugs, fishing vessels, freighters, ferries, cruise ships and pleasure craft are always traversing its length or breadth. The strait has an average depth of 155m (508 ft) and a maximum depth of 420 m (1378 ft) south of Texada Island.

The traditional lands of several Coast Salish First Nations, the shores of the Strait of Georgia currently is home to over 70 percent of BC's population. It's also the busiest overwintering spot for migrating waterfowl in Canada: 130 species of waterbirds visit the area annually. ∎

Top right: A very important waterway in the Pacific Northwest, the Strait of Juan de Fuca is a 100-nautical mile-long inlet stretching from the Pacific Ocean to Whidbey Island. Ships from around the world arrive at and leave from the ports of the Inside Passage via the Strait of Juan de Fuca. This couple is hoping to see whales at sunset near Limekiln State Park, on San Juan Island, the only designated whale watching park in the world.

Bottom right: Hotel de Haro at Roche Harbor, San Juan Island, was built in 1886. It's a popular resort for both mariners and land-based travellers. Teddy Roosevelt was a guest and John Wayne's boat is still tied up in the marina. The San Juan Islands' other famous resort is Rosario Beach Resort on Orcas Island, built by Seattle millionaire Robert Moran in 1909.

The Pig War

San Juan Island is not only the biggest of the San Juan group but it may have the edge on the others historically as well. Tensions ran high in this area when the British and Americans were trying to define the international boundary in 1859. Although 17 Americans were farming on San Juan Island at that time, some say they had been sent there to undermine the Hudson's Bay Company's claim on it for England. When American settler Lyman Cutlar found a British pig destroying his potatoes one fine summer morning, he shot the little porker. The British took offence and the dispute escalated. At the height of the tensions the British had five warships standing off-shore and the Americans brought several cannons to meet the challenge. The Pig War lasted 12 years, although no shots were ever fired. Kaiser Wilhelm of Germany was brought in to settle the dispute, which he did — in favour of the Americans. The odd dips and turns of the border in this area still leaves many residents scratching their heads. Today tourists visit the American Camp and the English Camp and wonder who could fight in such a beautiful spot.

Above: Artillery men at American Camp on San Juan Island during the Pig War, taken between 1857 and 1859. Although no shots were fired, canon balls still turn up in farmers' fields.

Arbutus

(Arbutus menziesii)

The only broadleaf evergreen tree in Canada, arbutus commonly grow along Pacific shorelines from California to BC. On the Inside Passage, they grow only in the Georgia Basin. Known as madrone in California and Oregon, these trees are distinctive because of their dramatically crooked shapes and paper thin layers of peeling brown bark.

Often seen precariously clutching onto rocky outcroppings, arbutus trees have the ability to survive the extremes of coastal weather. In the summer, they survive draughts by creating burls that store water for release when needed. When the burl's water runs out completely, the arbutus can let a branch or even part of the main trunk die off so that the tree can live: dead branches are common on many trees.

Normally reaching a maximum height of about 12 m (40 ft) and a diameter of 60 cm (2 ft), the largest arbutus in North America is found on Savary Island, at the northern end of the Georgia Basin. This giant is over 30 m (100 ft) tall. Growing nowhere else in Canada but on the moss-covered rocks of the Pacific coast, these trees can be found as far north as Seymour Narrows.

The arbutus' characteristic crooked shape comes

Opposite: Tourists have long been attracted to the Malaspina Galleries on Gabriola Island. The caves provide some of the most dramatic examples of sandstone sculptures in the world, reaching four m high and stretching 100 m along the shoreline. This excursion took place in the 1890s.
Left: An arbutus tree on San Juan Island.
Right: Heron Rocks, Hornby Island, looking south over the Strait of Georgia.

from its ability to grow horizontally and vertically as it clings to the rough terrain of the coast and bends around rocks and other trees for optimum sunlight. They are rarely seen beyond a kilometre from the shore.

The Arbutus has egg-shaped, shiny, dark green leaves. It is the only deciduous tree that does not lose its leaves in the winter. Although in early summer new leaves grow and the old ones fall off, it is never bare. As hardy as this species is, it is currently under threat by Sudden Oak Death (SOD) disease.

One Coast Salish legend says that the roots of the arbutus hold the earth together. Another legend tells how, in the great flood, people were able to survive by tying their canoes to a huge arbutus tree on a Vancouver Island mountain. The people were so grateful that they forbade burning arbutus wood for fires. ■

Barbara Hodgson,

Ham Radio Enthusiast, Sidney BC

Our motor has died just outside the harbour in Wrangell, Alaska. Luckily it's a rare calm day in June: the sun is shining, the water is flat, the wind is on vacation. As we are slowly towed behind the breakwater, we worry about finding space.

Crab season is about to open and the harbour is packed with commercial vessels, two, three, and even four deep along the dock in some places. As we inch alongside a powerboat to raft up, an energetic blond fifty-something woman with an unmistakable English accent shouts out a friendly "We've got you!" and reaches out for our lines.

Barbara Hodgson and her husband Gerry have travelled up the Inside Passage from their home in Sidney on Vancouver Island many times over the past 40 years. They invite us aboard their newly remodelled 35-foot power boat, the *MV Kluane*, and proudly show off the result of months of hard work. Barbara's pride and joy is her Ham station — and we're not talking food. Down a few steps from the main salon, she gestures to a collection of very serious looking radios with many dials, level indicators, logbooks, and auxilliary equipment along a portion of one wall. It appears very intimidating, but Ham radio is Barbara Hodgson's passion.

Obtaining a Ham licence is notoriously difficult among boaters and many shy away from it. Hodgson nods sympathetically. "When Gerry suggested it to me about eight years ago, I thought he

Above: *Barbara and Gerry Hodgson aboard the MV Kluane.*

was cuckoo," she says. "I was totally intimidated and terrified. I had no clue about radio waves or any of that. And it's a whole different language."

After her first summer using her Ham out on the water, Barbara's cohorts at the BC Boaters Net commandeered her into being a controller. Since Ham is one-way radio, someone has to coordinate the boaters who call in. Members of the net take turns at the role. "My radio shack is across the hall from the bathroom in our home," Barbara recalls with a chuckle. "My first time as controller I was over there six times in five minutes before we started, I was so nervous."

Typically boaters on a Ham net will tune it to a frequency at a regular time for a "roll call". If someone doesn't check in, others on the net are put on alert. If a vessel misses consecutive roll calls, the coast guard is notified. Through the controller, participants also check on local

conditions with other boaters, share information, or just catch up. "It's social, but it's also about safety," she says.

Eight years later, Barbara feels right at home with Ham. She manages the scheduling of the seasonal BC Boaters Net and is in charge of the year-round Great Northern Boaters Net.

Gerry, who is Barbara's "technical director", is also involved, and the couple wonders what their lives would be like without Ham.

"As you get older, one is inclined to get sedate, less involved in things," she says. "This has become a way of life meeting people we would never have known otherwise." They track boaters from offshore as well as locals and now have friends around the world. Once for two weeks she even acted as a relay between a couple sailing in the Queen Charlotte Islands and their daughter, who was having problems in her love life. "The daughter would call me every day and bounce things off me," says Barbara, then I would call the parents every night on the Ham and let them know what was going on. I became a second mother; we're still very close."

Barbara and Gerry view their Ham cohorts as a community. "It's a wonderful hobby," she says, "especially when you get older. You have all these friends, you don't have to go out the door — and you don't have to have them for dinner!" Then she laughs, a wonderful throaty chuckle, and you know if you were a Ham operator who just blew in from Hawaii or Cape Caution and arrived at Barbara and Gerry's door, you'd get a big hug, a warm welcome and very likely dinner.

Above: *Mount Baker from Georgia Strait*

Volcanoes on the Inside Passage: Mount Baker

Volcanic activity occurs when large plates under the earth's surface, known as tectonic plates, collide and slide under one another in a process called subduction, an event that is also responsible for earthquakes. Both earthquakes and volcanoes have been major forces in shaping the landscape of the Inside Passage. While visitors to the area are not likely to experience either, the Inside Passage has several volcanoes along its shores, including Washington's Mount Baker.

A tremendous amount of energy results from the collision of tectonic plates. When volcanoes erupt, it is because the force of the collision has forced one plate deep into the earth. The tremendous heat causes rock to melt into magma, some of which rises to the surface as lava.

Seventy-five percent of the world's active and dormant volcanoes are located in an area called the "Ring of Fire", which arcs around the Pacific Ocean basin. (At present, about 1500 volcanoes are considered active worldwide.) The Ring of Fire stretches from New Zealand, along the eastern edge of Asia, north across the Aleutian Islands of Alaska, and south along the west coast of North and South America. The Pacific Plate is the common factor. In the northeastern Pacific Ocean the major plates that collide with the Pacific Plate are Juan de Fuca, Gorda, and North American.

Mount Baker is part of the Ring of Fire. The last time it erupted was in 1870, although there was some minor activity in 1975. It is one the youngest volcanoes in the Cascade Mountain Range: others include Mount Rainier near Seattle and Mount St. Helen's in southern Washington, which erupted quite dramatically in 1980.

The US Geological Survey says that volcanic activity began in the area of Mount Baker about one million years ago, but due to erosion, evidence of that is not obvious today. The Mount Baker visible to us began forming during the last ice age, between 30,000 and 10,000 years ago. It is the second most active volcano in the Cascade Range, but scientists are not making any public guesses as to when it might erupt again.

Mount Baker Snoqualmie National Forest is a popular recreation area. The summit of Mount Baker, at 3286 m (10,781 ft) above sea level, is located in Mount Baker Wilderness area. The forest covers 534,334 acres with 80 km (50 mi) of trails. Currently Mount Baker supports 32 km (20 mi) of active glaciers.

Although Nooksack people called it quck-sman-ik meaning "white mountain" and the Lummi people called it kulshan ("broken off"), Captain George Vancouver named it after Joseph Baker a member of his crew who first spotted its peak during their 1792 exploration of the area.

Left: The view across False Creek from Granville Island. Originally a large sandbar used by First Nations people for fishing, Granville Island became an industrial site in the 1920s. Today its public market, theatres, artists' studios, restaurants and many small independent shops attract over eight million visitors a year.
Right: The North Arm of the Fraser River, just before it empties into the Strait of Georgia.
Opposite: Vancouver skyline featuring False Creek.
Following pages: A sailing ship loads lumber on the Fraser River, near New Westminster, ca 1863.

Vancouver

Long considered the world's most beautiful city by many of its residents, like Seattle, Vancouver consistently rates highly on world lists of best places to live. Beautifully located, the city snuggles between mountains and seashore, making it a cosmopolitan centre with dozens of outdoor recreation opportunities close at hand.

At the beginning of the 20th century, Vancouver saw itself as an outpost of the British Empire with very strong ties to England. But the ensuing hundred years has seen some marked changes. A 2002 survey indicated that 40 percent of the city's population are from visible minorities, making it one of the most multi-cultural cities in the world. Visitors who take the time to explore, will find neighbourhoods that include Chinese, Punjabis, Greeks, Italians, Vietnamese and Ethiopians.

Coast Salish people had been living at various locations on the hospitable shores of Georgia Strait and the Fraser River in this area when British Captain George Vancouver and Spanish explorer Dionisio Alcala-Galiano met off Point Grey in 1792. Kitsilano, now a popular residential area of the city, takes its name from the chief of the First Nations people who once lived on the shores of Burrard Inlet.

Sixty years later, miners on the way to the rich Cariboo gold strikes in 1858 left a demand for lumber and supplies in their wake that saw the first sawmills built around Burrard Inlet in the 1860s. The city's earliest incarnation was the town of Granville, built next to Hastings Sawmill, although local residents referred to it as Gastown, in honour of Gassy Jack Deighton, a former sailor, miner, and customs agent who opened a bar and hotel in the area for the millworkers. Today, Gastown is a historic area of downtown Vancouver near the major cruise ship docks.

If logging was responsible for the first settlement, the Canadian Pacific Railway's announcement in 1885 that Vancouver would be the terminus of the new transcontinental railway was responsible for the incorporation of the City of Vancouver the next year. Logging, mining, and fishing became the economic core of the city that is now the largest in the province and the third largest urban area in Canada.

Although economically tied to BC's abundant natural resources, in the last half of the 20th century Vancouver also became a major player in Pacific Rim trade, tourism and finance. Its harbour hosts ships from around the world. Much of the Alaska cruise ship industry is based here, contributing over $508 million to the local economy in 2002. ■

Fraser River

The 1,399-km-long (869 mi) Fraser River plays an important role in the life of British Columbia, draining an area of 231,510 sq km (89,386 sq mi), or about one-quarter of the province. As a major salmon-spawning river and transportation route, it has historically been important to a number of First Nations. It's the longest river entirely in BC, and today nearly 65 percent of the province's population lives in its basin.

During peak spring runoff, the monthly flow can reach as high as 7,000 cu m (437 cu ft) per second, although that falls to 850 cu m (53 cu ft) per second in winter. It often has a milky appearance due to the high silt content, which is also responsible for the rich farmlands at its delta. Annual silt loads are estimated at 20 million tonnes, with at least three-quarters of that carried into the Strait of Georgia.

Simon Fraser explored the river in 1808 for the North West Company, although the impassable stretch he named Hell's Canyon, ruled it out as a fur trade route.

In 1857, miners discovered gold on its banks near present-day Hope, starting a stampede that continued to the Cariboo gold fields in 1858, which subsequently opened up the province to development and settlement.

Designated as a Canadian Heritage River, the Fraser supports five species of salmon. Since the main river is not dammed, some of these determined creatures manage to swim upstream over 1300 kilometres to spawn. Environmentalists are increasingly concerned about its health. In the 1990s it was considered one of the ten most endangered rivers in the province. Nonetheless, 10 million salmon return to this river system annually; it produces more salmon than any river in the world. Twenty-nine other species of fish live in the river, with another 87 living in the estuary. ■

Port of Vancouver

Area covered: Roberts Bank (US-Canada border) to Indian Arm (northeast of Vancouver)
Miles of coastline: 233 km (145 mi)
Hectares of water: 6,000
Hectares of land: 460
Total cargo traffic: (2001) 72.9 million tonnes
Foreign vessel arrivals: 2820
Destination of largest percentage of exports: Asia(62%)
Number of export nations: 90
Value of cargo: $29 billion
Main export: Coal (27.2 million tonnes)
Other major exports: grain (11.7 million tonnes), forest products (7.1 million tonnes), sulphur (5.2 million tonnes), potash (3.2 million tonnes), chemicals (2.1 million tonnes)
Rank in the world (total cargo volume): 26th
Rank in North America (total foreign exports): 1
Number of major terminals: 25
Number of railways: 4

First Nations Place Names

First Nations people had lived along the Inside Passage for centuries when Captain George Vancouver explored the area in 1792 and they had names for many of the geographical features, sometimes two or three names for the same thing. But George was the man with the pen. Among First Nations names that survive along the Inside Passage:

Kaien, the island where Prince Rupert is. It's a Tsimshian word for "foam", which is created in the water during certain tide actions.

Ketchikan, the first Alaska stop for many Inside Passage cruise ships, comes from a Tlingit word meaning "where the eagles' wings are".

Kitimat, a town at the end of Douglas Channel, south of Prince Rupert. Kitimat is a Tsimshian word meaning "people of the falling snow."

Metlakatla, the name of two First Nations settlements, one on Venn Passage near Prince Rupert, and one on Annette Island in Alaska. It's a Tsimshian word meaning "a passage between two bodies of salt water".

Mukilteo, a Washington state ferry terminal town north of Seattle, connecting the mainland with Whidbey Island. The name means "good meeting place" and it was used for potlatches and councils.

Nanaimo, the town on Vancouver Island, comes from a Coast Salish word, "sne-ny-mo", meaning "people of many names". Five different bands in the area had joined together for protection, living in this location.

Skeena (River), south of Prince Rupert, is a Tsimshian name meaning "divide". The Skeena is one of the three largest rivers on the Inside Passage.

Tacoma, a large city south of Seattle, comes from the word Coast Salish used to describe nearby Mount Rainier, "Tahoma", meaning "mother of waters".

George Vancouver,

Early British Explorer

Captain George Vancouver, for whom the city of Vancouver is named, was responsible for charting a great deal of the coastal areas between Puget Sound and Skagway. Although his personality apparently left something to be desired, he was, by all accounts an excellent surveyor: many of the Canadian Hydrographic Service's current marine charts use his observations and records.

He was born in 1757 in England and first came to the Pacific coast of North America as a midshipman on Captain James Cook's expeditions between 1776 and 1780. In 1791 he was given his own command and charged to survey the coast between California and Alaska and settle some pesky ownership disputes with Spain.

Above: The charting expeditions led by Captain George Vancouver, represented in this 1796 portrait, provided the base data for many of the navigational charts of the Inside Passage in use today.

By the time he got here in 1792, the Spanish were waiting for him, but many historians feel his explorations had the most significance. Although many geographic features have Spanish and Russian names, Vancouver is responsible for the majority of place names along the coast.

On his 297-tonne ship, the *Discovery*, Vancouver and his crew spent three summers mapping the coast and many offshore islands. Their explorations discouraged hope of finding a Northwest Passage. He returned to England in October of 1795 in declining health, and died in 1798 after preparing an account of his explorations, which was published shortly thereafter.

Early Ships and Shipping

Ships have traditionally provided the main mode of transportation for people along the Inside Passage. Many communities north of Vancouver Island still don't have road access and can be reached only by water or air. The vessels that provided marine services were vitally important to the people who lived and worked along this route.

Evidence exists to show the Haida and Alaskan Tlingit travelled the Inside Passage in sturdy ocean-going canoes before the advent of Europeans. In fact, as late as 1846, the Hudson's Bay Company (HBC) ran mail, freight, and passengers from Victoria across Puget Sound to the mainland using a canoe acquired from the Queen Charlotte Island Haida.

Early explorers arrived in sailing vessels. Some were quite small by today's standards: Quadra's *Santiago*, which sailed north from San Blas, Mexico in 1775 was just 11 m (36 ft). These sailing ships made amazing voyages, but the intricacies of the Inside Passage's inlets and channels challenged the best of them.

The first steamboat on the Inside Passage was the *SS Beaver*, a 31-m (102-ft) steam-powered sidewheeler that the HBC brought from England in 1836 to service its many coastal forts. The company ran the vessel north from Puget Sound as far as Tongass in Russian America (now Alaska) until 1874. In 1853, the Beaver was joined by the 37-m (122-ft) *SS Otter*.

Although the HBC dominated coastal shipping, a number of smaller companies sprang up beginning in the 1850s.

Above: *The Hudson's Bay Company's* SS Beaver *was the first steamboat to travel the waters of the Inside Passage. This 1870s photo shows her on Vancouver's Burrard Inlet after she had been sold by the HBC. She was wrecked in Vancouver Harbour in 1888 after long and faithful service.*

Entrepreneurs in the Puget Sound area, for example, developed the "Mosquito Fleet", small paddlewheelers offering local passenger and freight service.

In the 1880s, the HBC fleet combined with a smaller company to form the Canadian Pacific Navigation Company and in 1901 the Canadian Pacific Railway (CPR) took over. The CP line of elegant Princess ships carried freight, mail and passengers to innumerable stops between Seattle and Skagway, dominating the Inside Passage shipping trade until the 1950s (and ending its then-diminished service in 1981).

But CP was not without competitors, among them the Union Steamship Company, established in 1889, and the Alaska Steamship Company, formed in 1894. The Alaska Steamship Company joined the Princess ships in an express service, but the Union Steamship Company won the hearts of people by visiting isolated logging camps, fish canneries, —whaling stations, mining operations, villages and float houses. During its 70 years of operation Union Steamships ran 50 different ships and in all that time lost only six lives. Recent oral history of the Inside Passage is inextricably linked to the history of Union Steamships.

In 1910, the Grand Trunk Pacific Steamship Company

Left: Hauling a whale up the slip at the Whaling Station at Nanaimo.
Right: The Hudson's Bay Company's Bastion stands guard over Nanaimo harbour in 1888. The fortified post was built in 1853 after the discovery of coal.

(GTP), developed a line of "Prince" steamships to connect Seattle, Victoria and Vancouver to its railway terminus in Prince Rupert, competing with the CPR's "Princess" line. The company ended its Pacific coast operations in 1975.

A number of Christian "mission ships" also travelled the Inside Passage during the early 20th century. Vessels such as the *Columbia, Northern Cross, Glad Tidings,* and *Thomas Crosby* provided an important link to inhabitants of remote camps and communities from the 1890s to the 1960s.

The often treacherous conditions of the Inside Passage combined with the demands of schedules and business were a constant challenge to the captains of these vessels. Today government-run ferry systems, high-powered tugs, and small freight boats are among the many that provide services up and down the coast, but the early days of shipping created an exciting unparalleled era in the history of the Inside Passage. ∎

Nanaimo

The second largest city on Vancouver Island, this mid-island city hosts the oldest preserved Hudson's Bay Company fort in Canada, the Bastion, built in 1853. The company established a presence here in 1849, with the discovery of coal that expanded to several nearby areas, including Comox and Cumberland. The area sustained mines until the 1960s and area colliery workers wrote much of BC's most dramatic labour history. Nanaimo production peaked in 1923 at one million tonnes. Petroglyph Provincial Park is just south of town. Newcastle Island, once a coal mine, is now a popular marine park. ∎

BC Facts

Provincial Capital: Victoria
Population: 4,067,200
Area: 947,796 sq km (365,946 sq mi)
Motto: Splendor sine Occasu ("Splendor without diminishment")
Bird: Steller's jay
Flower: Pacific dogwood
Tree: Western red cedar
Gem: Jade

The Sunshine Coast

The 100-nautical-mile stretch along the east coast of the Georgia Basin north of Vancouver is known as the "Sunshine Coast." The name is a bit of a brag: although it gets more sunshine than Vancouver, it doesn't do as well as Victoria. But it's popular with artists, retirees and people looking for a slower pace of life within reasonable travel time from Vancouver. Tourists have also been flocking to the area since the late 1800s.

One of the more well known towns on the Sunshine Coast is Gibsons, which was the setting for The Beachcombers, a popular syndicated television show from 1971 to 1991. The village of Lund at the northern end of the Sunshine Coast is the western terminus of the Trans Canada Highway.

The full force of Inside Passage tides and currents can be seen at Skookumchuck Narrows, near the tiny town of Egmont. As tides change and the water rushes through the narrows, currents can reach speeds of 16 knots, creating spectacular whirlpools.

Powell River, the main industrial town, is the site of one of seven pulp and paper mills in the Georgia Basin. Forestry is an economic mainstay of the area.

The Shishalh (Sechelt) of the Coast Salish First Nations are the indigenous people. European settlers arrived in the 1880s. ■

Left: A quiet anchorage at Smugglers Cove on the Sunshine Coast.
Right: Waterfall in Desolation Sound. This group of islands and inlets at the northeast end of the Georgia Basin, was named by a grumpy George Vancouver. On June 27, 1792, he saw it this way: "[It] afforded not a single prospect that was pleasing to the eye, the smallest recreation on shore, no animal nor vegetable food, ... whence the place obtained the name of Desolation Sound." Today it's a popular destination for summer cruisers.

Harbour Seals

(Phoca vitulina richards)

Harbour seals are found in coastal waters, estuaries and river systems throughout the temperate Northern Hemisphere. The Pacific harbour seal, which inhabits the Inside Passage, is just one of five subspecies. They tend to stay within 20 km (12 mi) of shore, so they are a common sight on the water.

This subspecies may reach a length of 1.6 to 1.9 m (5.2 to 6.2 ft) and a weight of 60 - 120 kg (132 to 264 lbs), and its colour can range from silvery gray to black, with a spotted, speckle pattern. The harbour seal is considered a true (earless) seal, because it has no external earflaps as the sea lion does.

While the harbour seal is now the most common of all the temperate-water seals, between 1913 and 1970, Canadian government bounties and extensive hunting dramatically lowered the seal population. Today however, experts estimate that Pacific harbour seals are approaching historic levels and number about 350,000.

Hearing and sight are highly developed in harbour seals — they actually see and hear better under water than above the surface. Their large eyes, protected by oily "tears", help them to see in deep, dark waters, and their hearing is almost 14 times greater under water (160 khz)

Left: Point Atkinson Lighthouse stands at the north entrance to Burrard Inlet and Vancouver's harbour.
Right: Harbour seals at rest.

than above the surface (12 khz). Besides their phenomenal sight and hearing, the harbour seal may also use echolocation. Whiskers can be extended forward to "feel" or inspect unfamiliar shapes and surfaces, and are extremely important in low-light situations. Blind harbour seals have been known to thrive in the wild.

Seals were important to First Nations cultures. Although there was no seal clan, seals were a symbol wealth and prosperity. Meat was harvested for food, oil for fuel, and skins for floats in whaling. Seal designs are often incorporated into decorative work.

The harbour seal's chief predator is the orca (killer) whale. The seal must also be on the lookout for some shark species and humans. While the seal is protected against commercial exploitation, it is still hunted by some native populations and may be shot by fishers and aquaculture operators or become entangled in fishermen's nets. New threats to harbour seal populations are pollution and the reduction of their food stocks, as well as parasites and disease.

Phil Little,
Former Mission Boat Crew, Vancouver

In 1959, the year he graduated from high school, Phil Little saw a write-up in his church bulletin about the *MV Thomas Crosby*, the United Church mission boat that worked the Inside Passage between Smith Inlet and Prince Rupert. "I signed on July 1st," he says, and that was it." He began as a deckhand and quickly became the engineer/mate.

"It was one of the greatest experiences of my life," says Little, now semi-retired from the insurance business. He left the *Crosby* in 1962 and today travels the Inside Passage on his own 50-foot sailboat, but his time on the *Crosby* left a lasting impression. "I was 20 years old and engineer on this 72-foot boat. And the coast in those days was alive."

The *Crosby* was based in Ocean Falls, at a time when, like many other coastal communities that no longer exist, it was thriving. The mission boat sailed north and south of there to "any place that people lived": light houses, logging camps, and towns like Butedale, Klemtu, Rivers Inlet, Hartley Bay, and Namu.

"The light houses were really interesting in those days," he says, "Ivory Island, Dryad, the Estevan Group, Pointer Island. There's nothing there now," he says of Pointer Island, "just a light, but at that time, there were families all over the place. We always tried to arrive at four o'clock, so you could get dinner," he adds with a smile.

"Rivers Inlet was booming," he recalls. "The canneries weren't there anymore, but the gillnetting was booming. You'd go in there and you were dodging gill nets like you can't imagine. Wadhams, Good Hope, Goose Bay, RIC. At Dawson's Landing they had the best store I've ever been in. Everything you could ever want. Stuff hanging from the

Left: Phil Little now explores the coast aboard the SV Forever Young
Right: Egg Island Lighthouse on Queen Charlotte Sound, where Phil Little and a fellow crew member conducted a mission of mercy on a dark and stormy night in the 1960s.

ceilings. It was a great store."

While Little obviously enjoyed the vitality of the coast in the late 1950s and early 1960s, there were some dark moments. He recalls visiting a logging camp in Smith's Inlet one night when they received a radio call that the light house keeper on Egg Island was sick and needed to get to the hospital in Bella Bella.

"It was blowing sixty something," says Little. "And that light house had been washed away at least twice — just gone. And you're in a bit of a lee at Egg Island. It's not nice out there. But we went down, the deckhand and me.

"We have to put the skiff over and go in on the swell. And the lighthouse keeper has to jump off the rocks into the skiff. And he's sick. And you have to ride the swell just right and then get the backwash back out and then get the thing turned around and out of there. Then we have to run all the way up to Bella Bella. It was the worst night I've ever been out." But they made it. "The *Crosby* would drive into a head sea like you wouldn't believe,"

he says proudly.

March was the worst month on the coast, Little recalls. "It was terrible. They put gale warnings out the first and they never came down the whole month. But then April would come. And places started to come alive. The fish boats are heading north. Things are moving. They're getting the canneries ready. The herring season is underway. You'd go into Namu when the herring reduction plant was running and the sun would set. And it would just be this pink glow over the whole Namu, with the smoke and the steam and the smell coming out of there. Boats everywhere. The whole coast just came alive.

"It's sad to see now. It used to be about the small guy making a living. One guy, one boat. He could fish most of the year and make a life out of it. That's what's gone. That's what's disappeared. It's crazy.

"We call it progress but what have we progressed to? We've progressed to the place where the guy has a boat and he fishes one week a year? That's progress?"

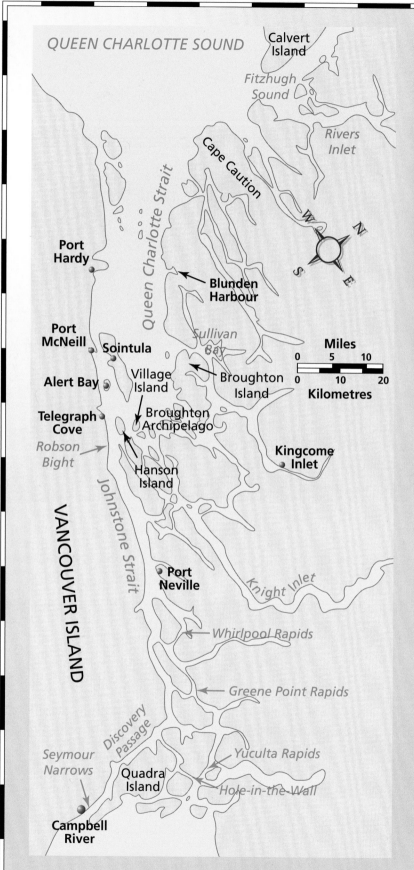

QUEEN CHARLOTTE SOUND

Calvert Island

Fitzhugh Sound

Rivers Inlet

Cape Caution

Queen Charlotte Strait

Port Hardy

Blunden Harbour

Port McNeill

Sointula

Sullivan Bay

Alert Bay

Village Island

Broughton Island

Telegraph Cove

Broughton Archipelago

Robson Bight

Hanson Island

Miles

0   5   10

0   10   20

Kilometres

Kingcome Inlet

VANCOUVER ISLAND

Johnstone Strait

Port Neville

Knight Inlet

Whirlpool Rapids

Greene Point Rapids

Discovery Passage

Seymour Narrows

Yuculta Rapids

Quadra Island

Hole-in-the-Wall

Campbell River

Above: *An arbutus tree clings to the rugged shoreline at Musket Cove.*
Left: *Map illustrating the Inside Passage from Campbell River to Queen Charlotte Sound.*

NORTHERN VANCOUVER ISLAND: DISCOVERY PASSAGE TO QUEEN CHARLOTTTE ISLAND SOUND

Above: *A misty morning at Port Neville on Johnstone Strait.*

North of Georgia Strait, the Inside Passage becomes more wilderness and less settlement. Campbell River, Port McNeill and Port Hardy are the major towns on the west side of this part of the passage, all connected by the Island Highway, which ends at Port Hardy. There is no road up the coast on the mainland: the Trans Canada Highway ends at Lund, south of Desolation Sound. The handful of small settlements on the east side of this leg have no road access to the outside world, making this waterway the major thoroughfare. While commercial vessels such as fishing boats, tugs, and ferries regularly travel this "marine highway", pleasure boats are less common, and the pace of life definitely slows.

The broad expanse of the Georgia Basin gives way to narrower passageways north of Georgia Strait, the inlets, fjords and islands offering clear evidence of receding glaciation. As tides ebb and flood, the water is pushed through narrow openings that create dangerous currents: captains of even the largest vessels always carefully consult their tide books. Currents at Seymour Narrows north of Campbell River can reach 16 knots, making it one of the most dangerous tidal passes in the world.

The weather too presents challenges, as the narrow passages also provide a funnel for winds, which commonly can blow 30 to 40 knots, more in the winter.

The main Inside Passage route is about 133 nautical miles, along Discovery Passage through the infamous Seymour Narrows, Johnstone Strait and then Queen Charlotte Strait to Cape Caution, but many vessels, particularly smaller ones, prefer "the back door" to Johnston Strait via Desolation Sound and its northern channels, thus avoiding the major shipping route. This route is not without navigational thrills, however, as currents in Dent, Yuculta, Arran and other rapids can reach 10 to 14 knots.

The action of large tides also creates an ideal environment for marine life. Rubbing beaches at Robson Bight on Johnstone Strait and elsewhere in this area attract whales. The area is also a flyway for migrating birds. A variety of land and marine mammals take advantage of local salmon runs for feeding.

First Nations Kwakwaka'wakw people have lived in this area for centuries and maintain strong cultural traditions to this day: the U'Mista Cultural Center in Alert Bay is a powerful place to visit. Uninhabited First Nations villages, petroglyphs, middens and totem poles are visible throughout this area, particularly in the islands of the Broughton Archipelago.

Johnstone Strait opens up into Queen Charlotte Sound and Queen Charlotte Strait, the gateway to the "Northern Canyons" and the first real wilderness of the Inside Passage. ∎

Left: A modern Salishan First Nations pole in Campbell River.

Right: Considered the Sportfishing Capitol of BC and the Salmon Capitol of the World, Campbell River has three major marinas that cater to both recreational and commercial boats.

Chinook weighing 14 kg (30 lb) or more from a rowboat using a hand reel and only one hook. Celebrities like Vincent Price, Tom Cruise, John Wayne, Bing Crosby, and Robert Duvall are among those who have tried their hands at bringing in the big ones. The club record is a 32-kg Tyee (71-lb) caught in 1968. ■

Discovery Passage

Named for Captain George Vancouver's vessel, Discovery Passage links the north end of Georgia Strait with Johnstone Strait through one of the world's most treacherous pieces of water (see "Ripple Rock", following). To the west is Vancouver Island and on the east lies Quadra Island. Pacific Ocean flood tides flowing in from both north and south meet just south of Cape Mudge on Quadra Island, creating treacherous sailing conditions when wind and tide are at odds. Discovery Passage is a haven for seabirds, sea lions and seals and has a world-wide reputation for its salmon sport-fishing. Cape Mudge is also notable as the home of the Kwagiulth Museum, which displays an impressive collection of previously confiscated potlatch items. The Kwakwaka'wakw settled here in the mid-19th century, displacing a Coast Salish First Nation group.

Across the passage from Cape Mudge is Campbell River. With a population of nearly 29,000, this is the major town on Northern Vancouver Island and considers itself the salmon capitol of the world. In 1924, local sport fishers started the Tyee Club; membership is limited to those who have caught a

≈Ripple Rock

On June 15, 1875 the sidewheel steamer *USS Saranac* was heading north along Discovery Passage through the Inside Passage to Sitka, Alaska on a low tide. The pilot aboard knew the dangers of passing through Seymour Narrows at the wrong time and advised the captain to wait for more favourable conditions: twin-peaked Ripple Rock lay just three metres under the surface at low tide. At the worst of times breakneck currents swirled around her and giant whirlpools yawned menacingly throughout the narrow (3 km long, .8 km wide) passage.

Apparently the captain of the *USS Saranac* refused his pilot's request, and soon after disaster struck. One account says the vessel hit Ripple Rock. Another says she got caught in a huge whirlpool. "All of a sudden," wrote *USS Saranac* seaman Charles Sadilek, who was aboard at the time, "there came a crash that shook the ship as if it had been fired into a battery of guns." The vessel went over on her side, but was able to head close to shore and anchor. Soon after the last man made it to safety, the vessel went down in 53 fathoms of water.

This was the first recorded shipwreck in Seymour

Narrows, but it is safe to assume there were others. In 1792 Captain George Vancouver had called it "one of the vilest stretches of water in the world." It was a reputation that stuck. Between 1875 and 1953, Seymour Narrows claimed another 119 ships and 114 lives. Petitions were sent to the government. Debates raged. In the 1940s two unsuccessful attempts were made to fix the danger. One resulted in the loss of nine lives.

Finally, in 1953, officials finally accepted a proposal to blast the top off Ripple Rock, requiring the construction of a tunnel under the water from Maud Island. Seventy-five men working in three shifts started work on the tunnel in 1955. It took them 27 months to complete at a cost of over $3.1 million. When they had finished, they had built a 174-m (570-foot) shaft on Maud Island, a 762 m (2500-foot) tunnel under the ocean floor, and two 91 m (300-foot) shafts into each of Ripple Rock's spires.

All the while, local residents worried. The explosion would take 1375 tonnes of Nitramex 2H and create the world's largest non-nuclear explosion. People feared earthquakes and tidal waves. They worried about destruction of a nearby mill and dam. On the day of the blast the RCMP would evacuate all residents within a three-mile radius.

At 9:31 on the morning of April 5, 1958, Ministry of Public Works consulting engineer Dr. Victor Dolmage detonated the explosives. The blast shot 370,000 tonnes of pulverized rock 305 m (1000 ft) into the air and displaced 320,000 tonnes of water, almost draining nearby Menzies Bay. But the earthquakes and tidal wave didn't materialize. In a few minutes the dust had literally settled and the new charted depth of Ripple Rock was 15 m (47 ft). Locals didn't feel a thing.

Although a much safer transit today, Seymour Narrows still requires careful navigation. Sixteen-knot currents rush through the channel at their maximum speed, and menacing whirlpools still twist and rage. Even the mega-cruise ships plan their transits close around the tides, giving this water the respect it deserves. ■

Johnstone Strait

A narrow 62-nautical-mile passageway that connects Discovery Passage to Queen Charlotte Strait, Johnstone Strait is lined with high mountain peaks; some on the south shore are snow covered year round. Although orcas, or killer whales, live in oceans around the world, Johnstone Strait is considered one of the prime viewing areas. Hanson Island, the north shore of Johnstone Strait, is the home of Dr. Paul Spong's OrcaLab, a renowned research centre.

The strait was named by Captain George Vancouver during his charting expedition of 1792, for James Johnstone, who was master of the *SS Chatham*, the second ship in the expedition. Johnstone led the group that discovered this sheltered passage to the Pacific Ocean in the north.

With Japanese military expansion in the 1930s, the

A Naturalist's Diary

"Two new species of Vaccinium was pretty common in the woods & grew in some places to upwards of 12 feet high, the one had large black berries & the other red — which were now beginning to ripen, & as they posessd a gratefull acidity we found them extremely pleasant & palatable after being so long upon salt provision. The only other fruit which the woods at this time afforded us was a new species of Rasberry that grew at least to ten feet high, & of which there were two varieties, one with a large red fruit & another with a yellow that were both equally grateful & pleasant but were not met within any great abundance. These Fruits together with a daily supply of fresh Spruce Beer greatly assisted to correct the bad tendency of our present mode of living."

Archibald Menzies, biologist and ship's doctor on Vancouver's expedition, anchored off Hanson Island, July 21, 1792.

Above: *Robson Bight Ecological Reserve consists of 1248-marine and 505-shoreline hectares. It was created to protect a core orca whale habitat for research and education and allows no public access.*
Opposite: *The traditional home of the Kwakwaka'wakw, Johnstone Strait was the site of several First Nations settlements. The village of Salmon River, shown here in 1890, is close to the logging town of Kelsey Bay.*

Canadian government worried about its vulnerable Pacific Coast and built a fort on Yorke Island (east of Kelsey Bay) in Johnstone Strait in 1937. Initially armed with two pre-World War I 120 mm guns and 55 men, after the attack on Pearl Harbour, the fort was expanded to include 260 personnel, 62 buildings, ammunition bunkers, searchlights and more modern weapons. Little remains today.

The Cracroft Islands, just south of Hanson Island, were named after Sophia Cracroft, who was the niece of Sir John Franklin, the explorer who died looking for the Northwest Passage in 1847. Sophia was companion to Lady Franklin, who continued searching for her husband long after he was reported missing. ■

Pacific Salmon *(Oncorhynchus)*

Above: On the beach in Alert Bay a Kwakwaka'wakw elder prepares salmon for a high school graduation celebration.

Pacific salmon, with their easily recognizable silvery sheen and spotted back and fins, have always been vital to life in the Pacific Northwest and are part of a heritage Canada shares with the United States. Several million Pacific Salmon appear along the coastline each year, most on spawning migrations. There are five species of salmon indigenous to the Inside Passage; chinook (or king), silver (or coho), red (or sockeye), pink (or humpback) and chum (or dog salmon).

The Pacific Salmon is an anadromous fish, meaning it spends varying portions of its life in both fresh water and the ocean. Each of the five species of Pacific Salmon differs in its life history, with pinks, for example, living only two years and reaching weights of two or three kg, while the giant chinook can reach over 40 kg and lives for up to seven years.

Salmon are born in gravel beds in freshwater streams up to 2000 km from the sea and spend the first part of their lives in freshwater, moving downstream to the food-rich waters of the Pacific Ocean the following spring. In early summer of their maturing year, guided largely by smell, they begin to head back to the streams where they were hatched. This voyage can last for weeks or even months as the salmon struggle against rapids, falls, and other obstructions. Their bodies now brightly coloured and distorted as they prepare for spawning, the males battle for the right to fertilize the females, and the female digs a redd in the gravel where she will lay up to 15,000 eggs. With spawning over, the salmon's life is complete, and within a short time it dies and the body nourishes the river and the nearby forest. In time the eggs hatch, and a new generation begins the cycle.

Because of this, salmon serve as a symbol of regeneration, self-sacrifice and perseverance in First Nations cultures. Many legends and rituals link low salmon runs to a lack of proper respect paid by humans. One custom of respect requires putting salmon bones back in the rivers or the sea after eating the flesh. One theory says that women are given high status in Northwest Native cultures because of their involvement in the salmon economy: preparing the salmon required more skill than catching it and thus women were the guardians of the most valued resource. Because of the important role salmon played in the lives of First Nations people, it is featured prominently in their art.

Today salmon are a valued part of all Inside Passage people and the management of the resource is an ongoing concern to everyone.

Lorna Hansen Chesluk,

Postmistress, Port Neville

"I've lived here for 51 years," says Lorna Hansen Chesluk, postmistress at Port Neville off Johnstone Strait. There's no town here, not even a store, just the post office. Across the inlet smoke curls up from a lone house; in the summers recreational boaters stop by. But it's pretty isolated.

Lorna doesn't mind. In fact, she loves it. "There's just something about the place — its beauty. Nature. I get up in the morning and stand here and look out this window across the water and every day I see something different." She picks up her binoculars and peers across the water, then passes them over. As if on cue, a deer strolls along the shore. "I could look out here all day," she says with a smile. "Never get anything done."

Lorna's grandfather homesteaded the 119-acre property in 1916 and Hansen family members have lived here ever since. Her grandfather was the first postmaster, then her father, then her mother, now her. Business, of course, is a lot slower than in the early days. When loggers and fishermen were more plentiful, there was also a store that sold supplies of all kinds — everything from chains to chutney — but it closed in 1960. Now the old log building is a kind of museum and gallery, a memory of a time when resource extraction was the lifeblood of coastal communities. Today visiting boaters marvel at its solid construction, admire the displays and buy books or local artwork.

Lorna lives here with her daughter Erica. Together they caretake the place for the rest of the family. Although she'll finish high school in Campbell River, Erica has been home schooled for most of her education. She publishes a quarterly

Left: *Lorna and Erica Chesluk outside the original log building that once housed the post office.*
Right: *A special relationship has developed between the local deer and the Chesluks. Here Erica feeds Rainbow Star, who is about to foal.*

newsletter that friends and passing boaters subscribe to that speaks well of home schooling. Teenaged Erica also connects strongly to the world around her, especially the animal world. She's given all the animals names, but you can tell that the deer (who are so tame they'll come when called and eat out of Erica's hand) are special. Erica and Lorna are particularly protective of Rainbow Shine, a nine-year-old doe due to foal any day.

One evening about 10 years ago, when Erica and Lorna were out for an evening stroll, a cougar leapt at Erica from behind a lilac bush. Lorna's scream startled the cougar enough that it missed Erica, and mother and daughter were able to run safely into their house. But Lorna's father, alerted by the commotion, ran out of his house in time

to see Rainbow Shine and a buck, on a hill above the clearing. The doe was trying to head down, as if to help Lorna and Erica, but the buck wouldn't let her pass, preventing the doe from coming down the hill and into some serious cougar trouble.

Although the Chesluks have help from a brother in Campbell River, it's a tough life for a woman, making ends meet, keeping the buildings and generator together, raising a daughter, fending off cougars, bear and wolves but she can't imagine leaving. "I like it here," she says. "If my grandfather could do it, why can't I?" Out the window, two herons perch on pilings down the bay. A whale glides by in the smooth water. The deer munch on tender spring grass. The line forms on the right.

Crows and Ravens

BC is home to most of the world's northwestern crows. Measuring about 16 inches from beak to tail, crows (Corvus caurinus) are often found foraging in tidewater areas. These bold and noisy scavengers are seen as a nuisance by many, and, in fact, during the early part of the 20th century, the BC government offered a bounty for their feathery little hides.

The crow's larger brother, the raven (Corvus corax), is distinguished by a bigger bill, a low croaking voice (as opposed to a "caw") and a fringed ruff of throat feathers. Mature ravens measure 24 inches from beak to tail and love to soar through the air. Although considered shy, they are still conspicuous.

Raven plays an important role in coastal First Nations legends and mythology as a creator figure. He took many forms, among them the Transformer and the trickster. With magical powers that allowed him to change his form on a whim, he also loved to trick and tease with instructional, but sometimes disastrous, results. Raven is also an important crest or totem figure, having great prestige.

Above: Long recognized as clever birds, in 2002 crows astonished animal psychologists in England who observed the birds making and using tools in order to get food.
Opposite: This raven totem pole was photographed in Rivers Inlet in 1913.

Crow Court

In the summer of 1983, Pete and Nancy Ashenfelter rowed from Lopez Island, Washington to Ketchikan, Alaska in a 17-foot open dory. The retired couple took two-and-a-half months to cover the 1215 km (750 mi) trip, rowing eight to 16 hours a day. While they were travelling along Chancellor Channel on the "back-door" route to Johnstone Strait, they came across an amazing sight.

"The fog continued to lift, replaced not by the sun we had hoped for, but by a soft steady rain. "Listen!" Nancy had stopped rowing and was looking over her right shoulder as I turned toward her. "Do you hear talking?"

"I hear something, but I don't know that it's talking. Kind of a babbling. Where?"

"Up ahead on the shore. It must be those crows." Nancy was pointing to a low, small, rocky point just up channel. We stopped rowing to watch, the current idly carrying us toward the gathering.

On the point was a group of about eight crows. They formed a yard-wide circle that enclosed a single crow. They seemed oblivious to us as we drifted toward them. First one crow talked and then the group responded, not loudly, as when "cawing", but more in muted guttural tones Then another took a short talking lead, to be followed again by the deeper-throated mutterings of the group. By some signal after a particularly active group response, the circle opened up and the group made

threatening peckings toward the "defendant." In response, he waddled over toward the shore trees and stopped, about fifteen feet away and sort of hunkered down, stooped-winged, neither standing nor lying, saying nothing. One by one, the rest of the crows flew off, all silent. The lone crow remained until he dropped from our sight as we rowed on. Had he just been drummed out of the corps for some violation of crow code?

In King Solomon's Ring: New Light on Animal Ways, Konrad Lorenz tells about the judicial system he has observed among jackdaws and other corvids. Others too who have studied crows have written of their rather advanced communal systems that have included kangaroo courts for trial and punishment of offenders among their group. "I wonder if we've just seen a crow court?" Nancy asked.

"It sure looks that way to me," I responded. "Whatever he did must have been pretty bad. I wonder if they have punishment to fit the crime? I feel like we've seen an intimate part of birdland — crowland, actually. Do you suppose he gets time off for good behaviour? Does he have to leave the group, or just take a lower pecking number?"

(From *"Row to Alaska: By Wind and Oar"* by Pete and Nancy Ashenfelter. Reprinted by permission of Nancy Ashenfelter.)

Left: Sullivan Bay, now a marina with a number of floating summer homes, started in 1945 as a floatplane harbour and was the busiest on the coast in the 1950s.
Right: Sunset at Sullivan Bay on North Broughton Island off Sutlej Channel.

Broughton Archipelago

Often referred to as "the mainland" by locals, Broughton Archipelago is a scenic collection of islands and mainland inundated with coves, fjords, passageways and inlets. The large tides and strong currents that pulse through the passageways support a rich intertidal and marine life. The natural resources have attracted and supported Kwakwaka'wakw people since the retreat of the glaciers ten thousand years ago. Middens, petroglyphs, fallen totems, uninhabited villages and pictographs speak to their early residence.

Largely undiscovered by tourists, the archipelago is becoming an increasingly popular destination for eco-tourism. Recently, it has also become the focus of heated debate over its fish farm industry, which critics say is destroying the indigenous salmon species. Established in the mid-1980s, archipelago fish farms currently number about 27.

Non-natives began settling the area in the 1880s. Harbledown Island, visible to the northwest through Blackney Pass, was the site of a Chinese community in the 1890s and early 1900s, complete with Buddhist temple. One of the earliest settlers on Harbledown was a Kanaka, who arrived in 1885. Kanakas were recruited from the Hawaiian Islands by fur trading ships during the 18th and 19th centuries because of their excellent sailing skills. ■

Tim Motchman,
Woodcarver, Sointula

Tim Motchman sits at the stern of a converted fishing boat tied up to the dock at Sullivan Bay. It's a beautiful August day and as people stroll by on their way to the general store at this floating village, they stop to chat while Tim works on his latest carving, a sea otter bowl. He's got a few of his finished pieces out on display — some are completed commissions, some are his own inspirations, all are reflections of his experiences living on the coast for the past decade and a half.

His boat is his studio and he spends the summers at various locations around the Broughton Archipelago and Malcolm Island, chatting and carving while he sits under the canopy on the back. Sometimes the chatting turns into a job. "People are getting more confident in my work," he says, "and I'm getting commissions. Which is fine, because I have a family now. Right now I've got enough work to last me until May."

Tim's route to this spot on BC's Inside Passage and this point in his life has been circuitous. Born in Kenya, he grew up in Penticton in BC's Interior, where the area's many lakes and waterways spoke to him. "Instead of buying a car at 16," he says, "I bought a boat."

Sometime in the early 1980s he headed west for a kayaking trip. "My first day on the coast, I fell in love with it," he says. It was also the start of a journey that would see Motchman learn how to make his art a meaningful reflection of his life.

"When I arrived I had a kayak and a Swiss Army knife. I spent two years living out of the kayak, figuring out how to do it. I met a guy who really knew how to camp," he explains. "Driftwood and a tarp — not a tent. Fishing. Just buying coffee, flour, basics like that. I got to the point where I could live on $50 to

Above: Tim Motchman carving on the deck of his floating workshop.

$100 a month. It was really important to me."

And he taught himself how to carve. He pulls out an early piece, a tiny bird flying over a piece of driftwood, the whole thing probably no more than 8 to 10 cm tall. The piece is lovely, but almost abstract in its simplicity — quite a contrast to the life-size heron he recently completed, with its metre-wide wing span and intricate detailing.

In the eighties when the coastal resource industries were still thriving, times were good for a young man trying to live off the land. "I could go to Sointula with carvings, sell them, grub up, and go off for several months," he says. When money wasn't so easy to come by, he took odd jobs. For a while he was a caretaker at Dr. Paul Spong's OrcaLab on nearby Hanson Island.

From living closely with the ocean and the land, Motchman learned the skills and developed the sensibility that shapes his art and his life today. "All of my work is from

my experiences living on the coast. Everything is water-based," he acknowledges.

He gets his wood from a number of different sources, all environmentally friendly. "There's a lifetime of wood up here for carvers, if you know where to look," he admits. He scrounges through old logging blocks, where long-discarded misshapen pieces of yellow cedar are plentiful. He picks up scrap wood from a small mill on a nearby island. It's all local. Part of the environment that he reflects in his work.

Although he usually starts with a drawing, it's only so he knows where to start carving. "I don't really pay too much attention to it once I've started," he confesses. "You can always take the wood off, but you can't put it back on. Carving is very different from lots of things — you're not putting it together, you're getting rid of the excess." Kind of like Tim Motchman's life.

Top left: Tom Sewid says he was a "hell-raiser" before he was told by tribal elders that he would become the one to hold the history and tell the stories of his people. "You're not permitted to say 'no' to the Chief," Sewid explains. With two his dogs, Land Claims and Fish Bait, he has been showing visitors around Village Island since 1988.

Bottom left: An aged pole at the uninhabited village of Mamalilaculla on Village Island.

Right: As Tom Sewid cooks a traditional salmon meal for visitors to Village Island, he tells stories and legends of the Kwakwaka'wakw people.

Potlatch

Above: *Bags of flour are stacked high in preparation for a potlatch in Alert Bay. The date is unknown, likely between 1897 and 1921.*

Most First Nations people along the Northwest Coast had an important ceremony of gift-giving called the potlatch (coming from a Chinook word meaning "to give"). The potlatch was a celebration of important events in the community, usually held in the winter.

Invited guests came to feast, watch dancing, and listen to songs that marked important events. These events varied depending on the tradition of the nation involved, but might mark a birth, a death, a totem raising, an initiation or other change in the status of kin, for example. Since there was no written language, potlatch became important socially and legally as a way to transmit history, events, status, kinship and traditions. Thus witnessing these ceremonies was vitally important. In acknowledgement, chiefs gave guests elaborate gifts for witnessing and remembering.

Before the arrival of the fur traders, and before the Hudson's Bay Company set up trading posts, potlatching was mostly practised by northern groups. But once a European economy was introduced into First Nations culture, trading became more prevalent, a new system of wealth was introduced, new tools were available, and warfare decreased. Gift giving became more elaborate and more competitive. Some say this resulted in a "golden age" of Northwest Coast Native art.

But European settlers didn't see it as a golden age. In fact they didn't understand the potlatch at all. What they saw were stacks of blankets, pots and pans, and other goods piled high on docks and beaches, goods that were just to be given away for the creation of status. Such behaviour, reasoned government officials and missionaries, could only lead to no good. Thus, beginning in 1884, the Canadian government banned the potlatch, making it illegal until 1951 when it was dropped from the Indian Act.

First Nations people continued to hold clandestine potlatches during this time. Dan Cranmer defiantly held a famous "Last Potlatch" on Village Island in the Broughton Archipelago in December 1921. Twenty six people were jailed. Many sacred, traditional and valuable artifacts were confiscated and sold to museums or private collectors. With a legitimate and traditional means of passing along important cultural information declared illegal, serious damage was done to Northwest Coast cultures.

In recent decades a concerted effort by First Nations people has resulted in the return of many of these artifacts and a regeneration of traditions and artistic expression. The U'Mista Cultural Center in Alert Bay and the Kwagiulth Museum at Cape Mudge near Campbell River both have collections that celebrate the reclamation and return of cultural traditions.

≈Alert Bay

Although it is named for the British warship HMS Alert that had been used in surveying the coast, this Cormorant Island community had been a seasonal Kwakwaka'wakw gathering place for centuries before George Vancouver sailed by in 1792. It became a permanent settlement when a saltery was built here in 1870 and First Nations people from Northern Vancouver Island moved here to provide a labour force. In 1890 the federal Indian agency moved in from Fort Rupert (near present-day Port Hardy) and in 1894 a residential school was built. The addition of a hospital, communications link, and commercial fishing and logging industries helped make Alert Bay an important centre during the early part of the 20th century.

Although the local economy has been depressed by the downturn in logging and commercial fishing, tourism opportunities are presenting new options for local residents. The 'Namgis First Nation operates the U'mista Cultural Centre, overseeing a very moving collection of reclaimed potlatch masks, robes and other artifacts. ■

Broughton Strait

Broughton Strait is a short stretch of water to the south of Queen Charlotte Strait protected by 83 sq km (32 sq mi) Malcolm and 3 sq km (1 sq mi) Cormorant islands. Telegraph Cove, Alert Bay, Sointula and Port McNeill are among the communities along this waterway, marked by tricky tides and heavy marine traffic, including ferries from Vancouver Island. The swift currents in the area create wildlife-rich channels that attract sports fishers, divers, and kayakers, making the strait excellent for wildlife viewing. ■

Spanish Place Names

The first confirmed contacts between First Nations people and Europeans were made when Spanish explorers arrived between 1774 and 1775. Spain was concerned with protecting New Spain (Mexico) from Russia and also wanted to find the Northwest Passage. Many places along the Inside Passage are named by or for these early explorers, among them:

Camano Island, Washington, **Caamaño Sound,** BC and **Caamano Point**, Alaska were named for Lieutenant Don Jacinto Caamano, who explored much of the coast north of the Strait of Juan de Fuca for Spain in 1792.

Galiano Island in BC's Gulf Islands was visited by Dionisio Alcala-Galiano in 1792, when he also met George Vancouver in a historic rendezvous off Point Grey, the site of the present city of Vancouver.

Malaspina Strait, BC, honours Alejandro Malaspina. Although born in Parma (now Italy), he was a Spanish subject. He sailed the coast of the Pacific Northwest in 1791, looking for the North West Passage.

Quadra Island, the eastern boundary of Discovery Passage, was originally called Valdes Island, but was renamed in 1903 for Juan Francisco de la Bodega Y Quadra, who, although born in Lima, Peru, explored the northwest coast for Spain, between 1775 and 1792.

Revillagigedo Channel and **Island,** Alaska were named in 1792 for a Spanish soldier, Don Juan Vincente de Geumes Pacheco de Padilla Horcasitas, Count of Revilla Gigedo, who rose through the ranks to become Viceroy of Mexico between 1788 and 1794.

Strait of Juan de Fuca was named for a Greek pilot, Apostolos Valerianos, who took the name Juan de Fuca. He may or may not have explored it for Spain in 1592 — historians disagree.

Sointula: A Utopian Experiment

Remoteness and isolation characterize many areas along the Inside Passage. For some that just makes it a nice place to visit. But others see the isolation and remoteness as ideal for settlement, and history records several attempts at creating Utopian communities along these shores. Such was the case with a group of Finns who founded Sointula on Malcolm Island at the beginning of the 20th century.

A Finnish word meaning "harmony," the Sointula idealists were led by socialist Matti Kurikka who had been invited by immigrant Finns who had become disenchanted with life in the coal mines of Vancouver Island.

The Kalevan Kansa Colonization Company was given a land grant by the BC government in 1901 and over the next three years attracted about 2000 settlers, although the actual number of people in the community at any one time was about 300. Despite hard work, the community's attempts at farming and logging were doomed to failure. For one thing, the island's soil and climate couldn't support cattle, grain or dairy production. For another, most of the settlers did not possess the skills needed to carve a community out of the wilderness: they tended instead to be poets, teachers, scholars and miners.

They did manage to publish the first Finish-language newspaper in Canada among other successful ventures.

Above: The present-day village of Sointula
Opposite: The village of Sointula ca 1910. The Finnish idealists tried everything from farming to newspaper publishing, but were unable to meet the challenges of combining Utopian principles with wilderness living.

But such enterprise wasn't enough. Financially unprepared, the community quickly became burdened with a debt they could not pay. Many people came to the community, stayed for a few weeks, and then left, leaving a huge burden on a small core group. There were disputes about private versus communal ownership, equal work loads, and decision making. Finally a series of disasters struck the community, including a fire in 1903 that killed eleven people. In 1904, suffering from the disparity between good ideas and impractical application, Kurikka left. In 1905 a shipment of desperately needed lumber was seized by creditors in Vancouver. In May of that year, the Kalevan Kansa Colonization Company was formally dissolved and the communal dream was abandoned.

But some settlers stayed on establishing individual homesteads and becoming loggers, fishers, and trades people, and the enterprising spirit continued. In 1931 a Sointula Finn invented the gillnet drum, revolutionizing the fishing industry.

Today Sointula is a charming community with about 700 residents and a Finnish flavour.

Above: These early settlers, known as pre-emptors, display a day's catch at Port Progress, now gone, on the mainland side of Queen Charlotte Strait.

Queen Charlotte Strait and Queen Charlotte Sound

About 15 miles wide, Queen Charlotte Strait can be a sobering sight to small vessel operators emerging from the sheltered waters of Discovery Passage and Johnstone Strait. The protective shield of the Insular Mountains begins to disappear at the southern end of the strait, until finally the wide open waters of Queen Charlotte Sound, stretching 175 km from the north end of Vancouver Island to the south end of the Queen Charlotte Islands (Haida Gwaii), present no protection at all.

Queen Charlotte Sound is one of the two stretches of open water on the Inside Passage. Winds come from every direction. Tides flow out of inlets, around islets, and over ocean floor contours, producing rips and currents far from shore.

Considered the dividing line between the north and south coasts of BC, it's the first big psychological hurdle for recreational boaters: passing Cape Caution safely is almost a rite of initiation. And everyone has a story to tell about making it across "the pond". ∎

Sam Cook,
Tug Boat Company Owner, Alert Bay

Left: *The* MV Cape Cook
Right: *Sam Cook aboard his tug,* Broughton Scout.

"It's my pa's," says Sam Cook of the *MV Cape Cook*, a trim, well maintained fishing vessel tied to the dock at Alert Bay Boat Harbour. The cabin is vertical boards, golden coloured, fir probably. But the stern is a big empty space where the fishing apparatus stood in better days — days when there was a salmon fishery. The *MV Cape Cook* has been in the Cook family for three generations, but she doesn't fish anymore.

The Cook family of Alert Bay is First Nations — they can trace their ancestors back to Nootka Sound on the west coast of Vancouver Island. That's where the legendary Captain James Cook made an historic landfall in 1778. They may be related. In any case, the family's relationship to fishing goes way back.

"We probably blew it," admits Sam Cook, glancing at the Cape Cook, "by trying to keep upgrading her." He points at the *Western Moon* and *Numas-1*, larger more state-of-the-art seiners that tower on either side. It would take Sam's family a day to haul in 50,000 pounds of fish on the Cape Cook; the more modern vessels could pull in that amount in an hour and be back fishing while the Cape Cook crew was still hauling in their nets.

Cook says that at one time out of the 500 salmon boats on the coast, 200 fished out of Alert Bay. Now there are maybe a couple of dozen tied up at the docks. "Of those," says Cook, "maybe five are licensed." The rest of the boats just sit there, virtually worthless: there's no market for the fish they could catch.

"A lot of people want to blame the demise of the salmon fishery on the fact that the boats got bigger and more efficient," says Cook, "but that's only part of the story."

Some people blame fish farms for the salmon fishery's woes. But he doesn't think that's really it either. "We like to do a lot of government bashing here," he admits with a grin, "but the truth is the demise of the salmon fishery is due to mismanagement. It's just cheaper to manage two days of a fishery than 20 days."

People get greedy under those conditions, Cook says. And they start working harder, trying to pull in more fish. "And everybody's working against each other, no one's working together."

Cook cashed in his investment when the government offered to buy salmon licenses. "They gave us 30 days to make up our minds," he says. Not much time for a livelihood that goes back generations. But he opted to get out. "I got 50 cents on the dollar and was glad to get it." And he was able to sell his boat.

Not so with the *Cape Cook*. "We probably put a million dollars into that boat, trying to keep it competitive. But no one will pay us that." So Sam's dad has been running a small-scale tourist operation out of it — sightseeing, fishing for dinner, that sort of thing. This past winter Sam leased the boat from his dad to house crew on his tug boats. Instead of fishing, Sam now runs several tugs out of Alert Bay, mostly servicing fish farms.

The irony is not lost on him. "Some of the young fellows, they won't work for me," he says. "They see it as working with the enemy. But I've learned that the fish farm market and the wild salmon market are two different things."

Sam doesn't say so, but it seems attachment to old ways may be the biggest enemy of all. "I'd say 20 percent of the workers who come to work on the fish farms are from St. John's [Newfoundland]. They've had about 20 years to get used to the fact that the fishery is gone. They come out here and are glad to get the work. It's totally different than fishing off boats, but at least they're on the water."

Above: Port Hardy harbour provides one of the few safe refuges for vessels waiting for a break in the weather to cross Queen Charlotte Sound.
Opposite: Blunden Harbour, on the east side of Queen Charlotte Strait, was the site of a Kwakwaka'wakw village until residents were encouraged to resettle in Port Hardy in the 1960s. This photo was taken in 1901.

≈Port Hardy

The northernmost town on this portion of the Inside Passage, Port Hardy is the jumping-off point for many small vessels heading north — a last chance for supplies and a safe harbour to wait out bad weather.

Native cultures have flourished on Northern Vancouver Island for centuries. Bear Cove, which is also the southern terminus of the BC Ferries coastal service to Prince Rupert, is the oldest dated archeological site on the island: archeologists have been able to date their findings to about 8000 years ago. The town of Port Hardy was settled by Europeans in the early 1900s but enjoyed slow growth until a mining operation was established in the late 1960s; the mine closed in the mid-1990s. Today logging and fishing are important economically.

Just south of Port Hardy, Fort Rupert was built near a First Nations settlement by the Hudson's Bay Company because of nearby coal deposits in 1849. The mine only lasted a few years before it closed in favour of richer deposits discovered near Nanaimo, further to the south. ■

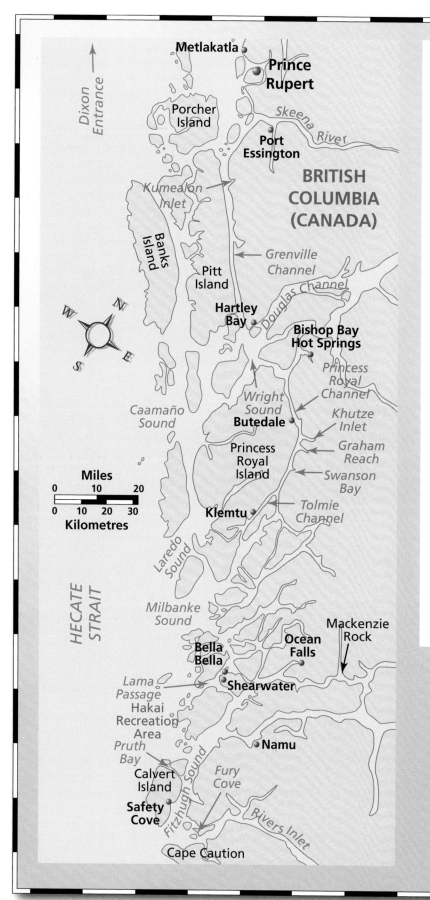

Metlakatla

Prince Rupert

Dixon Entrance

Porcher Island

Skeena River

Port Essington

Kumealon Inlet

BRITISH COLUMBIA (CANADA)

Banks Island

Grenville Channel

Pitt Island

Douglas Channel

Hartley Bay

Bishop Bay Hot Springs

Princess Royal Channel

Wright Sound

Khutze Inlet

Caamaño Sound

Butedale

Princess Royal Island

Graham Reach

Swanson Bay

Miles

0   10   20

0   10   20   30

Kilometres

Klemtu

Tolmie Channel

Laredo Sound

HECATE STRAIT

Milbanke Sound

Mackenzie Rock

Bella Bella

Ocean Falls

Lama Passage

Shearwater

Hakai Recreation Area

Pruth Bay

Namu

Calvert Island

Fury Cove

Safety Cove

Fitzhugh Sound

Rivers Inlet

Cape Caution

Chinook: A Lingua Franca

Chinook jargon was a pidgin language developed by First Nations people and fur traders from California to Alaska to facilitate communication. It used words borrowed from aboriginal languages, primarily Nuu-chah-nulth (Nootka), as well as English and French. With a total vocabulary of about 700 words, it was spoken by about 250,000 at one time, but its use has largely petered out. Some words, like *"saltchuck"* (ocean) and *"skookum"* (strong) remain in English slang. Here are some others:

Boston: English, white men
Cheechako: Newcomer
Delait: Very or very good
Hi yu: a huge amount
Hootchenoo: A kind of liquor
Hyas: Big, very
Klahowyah: Greetings
Klosh: Good
Kumtux: Know, understand
Mika: You, your
Poogh: Shooting
Sagh-a-yar: How do you do?
Skookum-house: Jail
Tillicum: Friend
Tola: To lead
Tucktay: Seaward
Tumtum: Mind, heart
Tyee: Chief
Wawa: Talk

Left: *Map illustrating the Inside Passage from Cape Caution to Prince Rupert.*

THE GREAT BEAR RAIN-FOREST: CAPE CAUTION TO PRINCE RUPERT

Once they have safely crossed the open waters of Queen Charlotte Sound, mariners always breathe a little easier. From here to Prince Rupert, the Inside Passage is a 386-km (240-mi) protected route through many inlets, narrows, reaches, and passages. Several regions along this route have been designated part of the Great Bear Rainforest, an area whose boundaries are vague at this writing, but has been defined as stretching from Kingcome Inlet in the south to Dixon Entrance in the north. A prime example of temperate coastal rainforest, the area has been targeted by environmentalists and industry, both of whom see it as important.

While this part of the Inside Passage is protected from the whims of Pacific Ocean weather, its channels present their own navigational challenges. High tides can reach 8.5 metres (28 ft) in places like Prince Rupert; winds can funnel down the channels at 30 or 40 knots and they cut through remote wilderness where towns are few and far between and the human population is sparse. In fact, some of the more remote areas have only recently received detailed charting by the Canadian Hydrographic Service.

First Nations people have lived on this section of the coast for thousands of years. Middens, petroglyphs, and other indicators hunker quietly in coves and inlets. Fury Cove on Penrose Island has a stunning shell beach, an ancient

Left: Passengers of the eco-tour SV Maple Leaf *experience the full brunt of Queen Charlotte Sound weather as they pass infamous Cape Caution. Cape Caution is considered the dividing line between the north and central coast of BC.*
Right: Detail of salmonberry, a common edible fruit found along the Inside Passage. Rubus spectabilis are an amber yellow relative of the raspberry found in the north temperate latitudes. The plant grows anywhere from 1 to 3 m (3 to 10 ft) tall, often in thickets.

repository of clam shells crushed by time. Near the abandoned cannery at Namu, archeologists have uncovered evidence of First Nations habitation at least 11,000 years ago.

In the middle part of the twentieth century the Northern Coast was a beehive of activity: fishing boats, canneries, logging shows and floating towns gave the area a vitality that is now relegated to memory and history books. Along the shores, legacies of this activity remain: a brick tower belonging to BC's first pulp mill peeks out behind trees at Swanson Bay, abandoned logging equipment lies rusting along Princess Royal Channel, the remains of a cannery sags into the water at Butedale. But modified logging and fishing continues, and the area is famous for remote fishing lodges, spectacular wilderness, and isolated pleasure cruising.

Environmentalists are also focused on this area. Despite the appearance of limitless wilderness, they are concerned about the maintenance of old growth forests and preservation of animal life. Through the efforts of First Nations,

Above: The wharf at McTavish Cannery, 1920. Rivers Inlet was once an active commercial fishing area, keeping 18 canneries busy. The first salmon cannery opened here in 1882. The canneries became redundant with improvement in refrigeration and freezing methods and the last cannery closed in 1950.
Opposite: Darby Channel connects Fitz Hugh Sound to Rivers Inlet north of Penrose Island, a provincial marine park.

environmental and local resident groups and the provincial government, the Great Bear Rain Forest was designated in 1990, stretching from northern Vancouver Island to the Alaska Panhandle. They hope it will form the heart of an initiative that will protect and revitalize this complex ecosystem. ∎

Fitz Hugh Sound

Fitz Hugh Sound is a narrow channel connecting Queen Charlotte Sound with Fisher Channel to the north, covering a distance of 65 km. Although once dotted with Heiltsuk First Nations villages, today there are no settlements along this part of the Inside Passage. The ancient village and former cannery town of Namu on the east side has a small caretaker population and Hakai Recreation Area on the west side attracts recreational boaters and sports fishers. The Sound was named by a fur trader, James Hanna, in 1786.

Although Fitz Hugh Sound provides shelter from the sometimes furious seas of Hecate Strait to the west, like other channels on the Inside Passage, winds can blow hard here. Namu, although in a sheltered bay, is a Heiltsuk word meaning "place of high winds". ∎

Above: *Rocks at West Beach, Calvert Island. Half of Calvert Island is in Hakai Recreation Area, a 1230 sq km marine park that borders the east side of Fitz Hugh Sound, including most of Hunter Island.*

Opposite top: *A busy cannery from 1893 to 1969, Namu (in 2002 on **left** and 1906 on **right**) also enjoys major archeological significance. Experts have found evidence that the site has been used by First Nations people for at least 11,000 years, making it the oldest recorded place of human settlement on the BC coast. It is also the longest continually occupied site in Canada.*

Mosquito Tree

Tree carvings and culturally modified trees occasionally appear in hidden spots along the Inside Passage. This tree carving of a mosquito is at Pruth Bay on Calvert Island.

Tlingit legend tells of an evil giant who was killed by a young man. Before he died, the giant said to the young man, "You can kill me, but I will still bite you. The young man killed the giant and threw the body on a fire. The ashes rose up in the air and came back down as mosquitoes that bit human flesh in revenge.

Right: Tree carving at Pruth Bay on Calvert Island

Joy & Lloyd Martin
Caretakers, Hakai Beach Resort, Calvert Island

Left: Joy and Lloyd Martin on the porch of their cabin at Pruth Bay.
Right: Pruth Bay, Calvert Island

Joy and Lloyd Martin have been caretakers of remote Hakai Beach Resort on Calvert Island since 2000, and Lloyd has only one disappointment. "I've never managed to find more than one or two prawns in my trap," he admits.

But the couple has managed to find a lot of other things. Originally from the Prairies (he from Saskatchewan, she from Alberta), the retired business people delight in their new occupation. "It's so nice to come here in September and leave the whole world behind," says Lloyd, as he shows off his collages — a jumble of shells, seaweed, starfish, driftwood and other beachcombing booty collected on the shores of Calvert Island's stunning beaches.

"Lloyd can't sit still," says Joy. "He's not ready to retire." And although one might think that watching over a remote fishing lodge from September to May might sound like retirement, Lloyd's not buying it. "I've never had a regular job," he says in the living room of their comfortable log caretakers' cottage that looks over Pruth Bay. "I've always had my own businesses — something on the go." And life is no different here.

He shows us the project for that day — adding a final coat of varnish to the lodge's circular wood dining tables. The summer crew will be arriving in a couple of weeks, so he's getting things ready. He points out the turnaround behind the lodge that he built over the winter so the staff will have an easier time loading and unloading supplies.

So enamored are they of their situation, the Martins are hard pressed to come up with a downside. "Challenges? I don't think there have been any," they both say. Lloyd doesn't count breaking his ankle last winter and setting it himself. And Joy doesn't count the fact that someone has to be at the resort all the time, which makes small escapes to Shearwater impossible for both of them at the same time. "The owners even offered to fly us out to Vancouver for a bit of a break," Joy shrugs, "but we didn't want to go." They both admit missing their grandchildren, whose pictures cover their three fridges and freezers. One suspects they make up for it during the summer when they're back visiting with family.

"I love the solitude," says Joy, "and enjoying nature." The island has a pack of resident wolves; one of them comes to visit Joy every day, sometimes two or three times. She has named it Wooffy, and to her surprise, Wooffy comes when she's called. "She won't come too close though," says Joy. "She always keeps about 40 or 50 yards away." Joy and Lloyd describe the activities of Wooffy and her male companion like proud parents, detailing, for example, how the two animals sat on the dock one winter night, nose to nose, howling at each other under a full moon.

The resident animals are not the only ones who provide surprises. As caretakers, Joy and Lloyd make it their business to know all the comings and goings of vessels in the bay. Anyone walking up the gangway from the dock is met with a friendly hello, directions to the beach, and a reminder to pick up after pets. They make you feel welcome, but also let you know they're aware you're around. So they were surprised one day, when, no boat in sight, a couple appeared "from nowhere," walking by their door.

"Where the hell did you come from?" asked a startled Lloyd. "San Diego," replied the couple. "They were rowing to Alaska — in an 18-foot boat with a collapsible mast," says Lloyd, shaking his head.

Joy remembers another boat that came in. "It was a family of four — two adults and two kids — in a 30-foot sailboat. They'd come all the way from Japan. Imagine."

The Martins are not sure how long they'll stay at Hakai Beach Resort, but when they leave, it won't be back to the big city. Or Saskatchewan. "We're thinking maybe the Queen Charlottes," says Joy. More solitude. More nature.

Above left: The power plant, one of the survivors when the provincial government closed the town, now provides power to Shearwater and Bella Bella.
Above right: This abandoned apartment building once housed Pakistani mill workers.
Left: Water spills over the dam from Link Lake in Ocean Falls.

Ocean Falls

Originally a Heiltsuk summer fishing camp at the end of Cousins Inlet off Fisher Channel, the Ocean Falls area was visited by Captain George Vancouver on his coastal explorations in 1793, but didn't really gain notice until the early 20th century when entrepreneurs decided it would be a great place for a mill.

The concept received support with varying degrees of success until 1916, when nearby Link Lake was dammed. From then until the 1970s the town was a coastal success story as various companies operated here, including the mighty Crown Zellerbach corporation, running a paper mill that produced everything from onion skin to toilet paper. The company also produced world class swimmers. When a child fell off the dock and drowned in the 1940s, management built a swimming pool and decreed that every child would learn to swim. In the 1950s and 1960s, Ocean Falls swimmers like Sandy Gilchrist were winning gold medals for Canada.

The town closed down in 1984 and by that time most of its heyday population of 4000 had left. Today it is a modern ghost town. The power plant is operational, supplying power to the coastal communities of Shearwater and Waglisla (Bella Bella), but the once-famous 300-room hotel and Hudson's Bay Company store, townhouse complex and most of the other remaining buildings are empty. The provincial government destroyed most of the Edwardian-style homes when it closed the town, but some remain, with the occasional peony and hydrangea poking through the weeds along the empty streets.

With an annual rainfall of about 330 cm [130 in], Ocean Falls developed a reputation as a very damp place to live. Many former residents, who were called "the raincoast people", have a great loyalty for their town even though it no longer exists, and come back to visit regularly. ∎

Top: *Ocean Falls residents celebrate Dominion Day in July 1919.*

Bottom: *An aerial view of the mostly abandoned town of Ocean Falls. Link Lake is in the background, the power plant in front.*

Alexander Mackenzie: "From Canada by Land"

Alexander Mackenzie was just a kid when he went to Montreal and joined the fur trading company that later became the legendary North West Company. Little did the fifteen-year old know that he was about to leave his mark in history by becoming the first non-aboriginal to cross the North American continent.

But leave his mark he did. Literally. On a rock just north of Ocean Falls on Dean Channel, he painted the words: "Alex Mackenzie from Canada by land 22nd July 1793."

Mackenzie left Montreal the previous year, in search of a great river that was rumoured to flow westward into the Pacific Ocean. (On an earlier attempt, he had followed the Mackenzie River to its mouth on the Arctic Circle.) Accompanying him was another trader, six French Canadian voyageurs and two Native hunters — all of them in a 25-foot canoe. It was an arduous journey, portaging and canoeing up one side of the Great Divide and down the other. After wintering at a fur-trading fort on the Peace River, they stashed their canoe and supplies on the impassable Fraser River and walked the remaining 300 miles to the coast, exhausted and short on food.

He was told by the Bella Bella that he had just missed meeting up with "Macubah" a fellow white man, undoubtedly Captain George Vancouver who had been charting the area in early June. Unfortunately for the Mackenzie party, that meant they had missed some good food (at least better than their depleted supplies), interesting conversation, and a ride south. The explorers were forced to turn around and go back the way they'd come.

Above left: Alexander Mackenzie, a Scottish orphan, made a historic passage across North America by land in 1793, several years before Lewis and Clark completed their famous journey in 1805.
Above right: A monument marking a significant historical event — Alexander Mackenzie's historic trek across North America — keeps a lonely watch over Dean Channel.
Below: Although the Mackenzie painted his original message in vermilion grease, his message has since been chiseled into the rock

The Mackenzie group made their historic journey a full 12 years before Lewis and Clark completed their famous trans-continental trek. The Americans seem to have secured a more visible place in history, but Mackenzie was widely acclaimed in his lifetime. He returned to England a celebrity in 1804, having published an account of his exploits in 1801, "Journey from Montreal." He died in Scotland in 1820.

Above: The village of Bella Bella on Lama Passage in the 1880s.

Right: During World War II, an ad hoc "gumboot army" made up of homesteaders, fishermen and loggers, patrolled the Inside Passage. Eventually the Royal Canadian Air Force built a reconnaisance base at Shearwater. This vintage hangar is now used by a boat building operation.

Opposite top: An eagle on its regular roost outside the Shearwater marina.

Bella Bella and Shearwater

Sometimes people in this area talk about Bella Bella/Shearwater as if it were one entity. In fact, they are two very different towns on Lama Passage just a five-minute water-taxi ride apart. Bella Bella, today called Waglisla, has a long history on the coast. The Hudson's Bay Company established Fort McLoughlin near here from 1833 to 1843, then reopened a trading store in 1868. The town grew up as people of the Heiltsuk nation settled near the trading post from outlying areas. (The *SS Beaver*, the first steamship in the North Pacific plying the coast in mid-19th century, arrived in Bella Bella in 1836.) In the 1890s, the townsite was moved, and it became known as New Bella Bella and later Waglisla. Today it is the home of the Heiltsuk nation, which operates a store and fuel dock. McLoughlin Bay, just south of the village, is a BC Ferry dock. Across Lama Passage sits the ruins of a cannery, once operated by BC Packers.

Shearwater was developed as an air force base from 1938 to 1942, one of several military installations built along the Inside Passage during World War II. Besides bomb shelters, mess halls and barracks, the RCAF built three large hangars here, one of which one remains today, housing a ship building operation. Shearwater has a marina/resort and the only vessel haul-out facility between Port Hardy and Prince Rupert. ∎

Tide Pools

One very accessible opportunity to observe wildlife on the Inside Passage is at the shoreline, where patience and a little information can reveal a bustling and complex ecosystem loaded with weird and wonderful creatures.

The Inside Passage normally experiences two tide cycles every day (actually every 24 hours and 50 minutes). The difference between high and low tides varies every cycle, but at some places along this coast, ranges exceeding 8.5 metres (28 ft) are not uncommon. (By comparison, in the South Pacific, the difference between high and low tide averages about one metre).

As the tides rise (flood) and fall (ebb) they alternately cover and expose an intertidal zone between the high tide mark and low water. When the intertidal zone is a rocky shore, the indentations in the rocks catch retreating sea water creating tide pools. Varying in depth from shallow puddles to deep holes, these tide pools support a variety of marine life.

The creatures that survive in these pools must be hardy and adaptable in order to survive the rigours of

Above: Tide pools support complex and fascinating ecosystems. Observers should be careful not to permanently disrupt tide pools or the creatures in them. Even displacing an animal by just a few metres can fatally remove it from its food source.

both wet and dry conditions, including elements like crashing waves, hot sun, churning currents and cold winds.

The flood tides bring fresh oxygen and food that sustain life in these pools. But during ebb tides, the creatures are exposed to the elements: some pools might dry out completely during a tidal cycle. Residents often find shelter under rocks or seaweed or just "close up" until the water returns.

Careful observation of a tide pool will reveal many different species, including sponges, corals, anemones, worms, chitons, snails, limpets, bivalves (like mussels, clams and oysters), barnacles, crabs, sea squirts, urchins and seastars. Tide pools also support a variety of seaweeds and grasses.

Close Encounter of the Whale Kind

Above and inset: Close encounter with a humpback whale.

Obtaining the perfect whale shot is always a challenge no matter how many sightings you make. On a calm, clear July morning on Finlayson Channel, just northeast of Klemtu, we noticed a whale spouting water off in the distance across the channel as we motored south. The whale was quite a ways off — a kilometre at least — but out came the telephoto lens.

Ron watched the whale through his lens and clicked away. At the helm, I kept an eye on the water ahead, looking out for deadheads and keeping us on course. Soon we realized that the whale was coming closer each time it resurfaced and we were on a collision course. We could see he was a humpback, about the same length as our 40-foot sailboat, but probably twice as heavy.

Humpies come north in the summer for feeding. Were we lunch? Although they tend to reproductive matters on their migrations south, we have, we feel, an awfully attractive boat. Was he viewing the hull as a potential mate? Or was he just having fun with the humans?

Whatever his intentions, he was not shy. All of a sudden he emerged very close to our boat, just two or three metres away, midship on the starboard side — a large, round, black shape quietly sliding up through the water.

He hung there suspended, his shiny black eye seeming to examine us, then quietly sunk below the surface of the water, barely causing a ripple.

He dove under the dinghy we were towing behind and then re-emerged on our port side, again just a couple of metres away. Barely a ripple, then the sound, a water-echo of gentle spray. The eye just looking, unfathomable.

Twice more the whale dove and hung, quietly peering at us. Each time it appeared and disappeared the water barely moved. Each time our awe increased, and we wondered if we should be afraid. Finally, he rose out of the water off our bow, then rolled away, giving the vessel a powerful slap with its tail as it dove deep below us.

He surfaced once more off the stern, then we saw his fluke disappear into our wake and he was gone.

Certain individual whales seem to have the "novelty seeking gene", a whale researcher from Simon Fraser University later told us. The same researcher also has observed that humpbacks in behavioural transitions tend to be investigative. If food isn't available, and the whale isn't ready to sleep or move on, they sometimes get playful with sea lions or kelp. Or boats with attractive hulls.

Finlayson Channel

The relatively short (24 nautical miles) waterway of Finlayson Channel marks the beginning of what has been described as "the Northern Canyons", a series of long narrow channels that make up the Inside Passage between Milbanke Sound northwest of Bella Bella and Chatham Sound south of Prince Rupert. The islands on both sides of Finlayson Channel — Dowager, Susan, Roderick and Princess Royal — rise to elevations of 457 to 793 m (1500 to 2600 ft).

During the summer months Finlayson Channel is susceptible to "red tide", a phenomenon that occurs when certain phytoplankton (microscopic, single-celled plants at the bottom of the food chain) species containing reddish pigments grow very fast, or "bloom", so that the water appears to be coloured red. Not associated with tides at all, red tide is usually not harmful, but a small number of species do contain potent neurotoxins, which can wreak havoc on the food chain. ∎

Left: Klemtu is the only currently occupied village in Kitasoo/Xai'xais territory. The people of Klemtu come from two different linguistic groups: the Tsimshian and the Kwakwaka'wakw.
Top and bottom left: *Forestry is still important to the economy of the Inside Passage. These loggers take it easy as they move down Finlayson Channel to a new job.*

Princess Royal Channel

With narrow widths, high mountain walls, and stunning waterfalls, this 61-nautical mile stretch of the Inside Passage is the heart of the Northern Canyons. Made up of several smaller channels — Graham Reach, Butedale and Malcolm passages, Fraser Reach and McKay Reach — Princess Royal Channel has no settlements, but lots of reminders of the glory days of logging camps and canneries. This is another place where tides flood in from both the north and south and meet somewhere in the middle — in this case in the vicinity of Aaltanhash Inlet, in Graham Reach. ∎

Hermann Meuter,
Whale Researcher,
Gil Island

Above: *Hermann Meuter and his dog at Port Neville, enroute to Gil Island.*

When Hermann Meuter was a little boy in Germany, he developed a fascination for whales. A decade or two later, after finishing university, he and a friend decided to travel the world. "The place I wanted to go was Canada," says Meuter. "I wanted to see a whale." And he did. "It was an amazing experience," says the research biologist. "I was hooked."

Meuter returned to Germany but retained his fascination for these huge creatures, the largest mammals on earth. He wrote to Dr. Paul Spong, an expert on Orca whales, who runs the Orca Lab on Hanson Island in Johnstone Strait, one of the world's more famous whale habitats. He was invited to join the Orca Lab crew and worked six months a year as an assistant at Dr. Spong's family-run lab. That lasted for ten years until he finally got tired of the commute and decided to live in Canada full time. In the summer of 2002, Meuter and his wife Janie were setting up their own research lab on remote Gil Island, off the northwest coast of Princess Royal Island.

The social structure of whales fascinates Meuter. "We can learn a lot from them," he says. "They are at the top of the food chain, but they are not aggressive."

He has developed a great deal of respect for the Gitga'at people in Hartley Bay, who have title to the land on Gil Island. He feels they are trying to do the best for their people and the environment at the same time, not always an easy task when corporations come in and offer them a million dollars for fish farming rights in their jurisdiction — an offer Meyer says the Gitga'at have turned down. "They're one of the few bands on the coast to do so."

Whale research has grown in leaps and bounds since its often dramatic beginnings in the 1970s, but Meuter notes there is still much to learn. He points out that migration patterns are well documented in Johnstone Strait, but little is known about where they go when they leave that area. "But it's impossible to study whales in the ocean on the north coast," says Meuter, "so our research will be land-based."

At the Cetacea Lab, the husband-and-wife team will be monitoring underwater microphones set at about a 50-mile radius from home base in order to track orca migration patterns. There are 200 orca whales in the Inside Passage, which have been broken down into three acoustic clans. "Each clan has totally different calls," says Meuter. The clans are broken down further into pods, and then families. Each of these subgroups also has their own distinguishing calls, while maintaining the identifying features of the larger group. While the meaning of some calls have been identified, such as excitement or resting, not all calls are understood by researchers. "We will probably never know everything about whales," says Meuter, "but that's as it should be."

While Meuter is obviously passionate about whales, he is not hard line about policies for their protection, opting instead for public education. "Whale watching is becoming more and more popular," he notes, "and we want people to understand their impact when they approach whales."

For example, when whales sleep they form "resting chains." These are difficult formations for the whales to get into and maintain, Meuter explains. Loud noises, such as outboard engines, can frighten them badly. Even kayakers who move silently through the water, can surprise a resting chain, and have a very negative impact on the whales.

Meuter also points out that by tracking whales on their migratory journeys, they can monitor the health of pods and even individual whales. Since whales are at the top of the food chain, their health is an indicator of the health of the ocean. The health of the ocean, of course, impacts us all.

Top: *A building at the former cannery town of Butedale, dramatically sags into the water.*
Bottom left: *A misty morning on Khutze Inlet, an isolated and beautiful anchorage off Graham Reach.*

Bottom right: *A piece of abandoned logging machinery, Princess Royal Channel.*

Great Bear Rainforest

Much of the Inside Passage is coastal temperate rainforest — typified by high mountain ranges looming over the ocean, creating copious amounts of precipitation. Originally, experts say, one-fifth of one percent of the world's forests were coastal temperate rainforest. Today, almost sixty percent of that is gone, as are half of North America's ancient coastal temperate rainforests. Some say they are more endangered than tropical rainforests, which have become a focus of environmental concern in recent years.

The health of the rainforest depends on the complicated interaction of four systems: terrestrial, freshwater, marine and estuarine. If one part of the system is threatened, damaged or destroyed, the whole system suffers.

Environmentalists, conservationists, scientists, First Nations, local communities and others have designated a 70,000 square kilometre area of BC's coastal temperate rainforest as the Great Bear Rainforest (GBR). One of the largest contiguous coastal temperate rain forests left in North America, possibly the world, the GBR stretches from Knight Inlet in the south to the Alaska Panhandle in the north, covering an area the size of Ireland.

Besides being home to eleven First Nations, the valley bottoms sustain more biomass than any other terrestrial ecosystem on Earth. The largest grizzly bears in Canada, the rare Kermode bear and genetically unique wolves are among the animals that roam through old stands of Sitka spruce and red cedar; some of the trees are estimated to be 800 to 1000 years old. Six million migratory birds are also sustained by the GBR.

One of the key species in this whole system is the wild salmon. All five Pacific salmon species spawn in the rivers and streams of the GBR. Not only is the salmon vitally important to First Nations cultures, but it provides food to other mammals like bears and wolves. When fish carcasses are discarded on the forest floor, they provide nutrients for insets and smaller mammals as well as to the soil and trees. Salmon are also a vital part of the marine cycle, feeding on and being eaten by other species. The health of the salmon run is an indicator of the health of the entire ecosystem.

About 2.5 million hectares is roadless, pristine wilderness. In April 2001, as a result of cooperative efforts by stakeholders, the provincial government agreed to restrict development of 20 watersheds and place a moratorium on another 68 large valleys in this area of the GBR.

While the idea of such a massive protected area seems progressive and farsighted, advocates of the Great Bear Rainforest are disappointed that, at this writing, the government has not moved to turn its designation into legislation. Concerned that time is running out, they see continued clearcut logging and an increase in ocean pen fish farming as threats to the well being of this system.

Top left: *Waterfall, Bishop Bay*

Top right: *Bunchberry* (Cornus canadensis), *also known as ground dogberry, is the smallest dogwood, growing to only about 8 inches tall. A common species in temperate rainforests, a group of these plants can look like a miniature dogwood forest, if you get your eye very close to the ground. Their red berries are eaten by a variety of wildlife including crows, squirrels and bears.*

Bottom right: *Western yew* (Taxus brevifolia) *is the only species native to BC. Traditional uses of its strong resilient wood by First Nations include paddles and bows.*

Opposite: *The Great Bear Rain Forest is the only place in the world where the rare white Kermode bear live. Actually a subspecies of the black bear, these all-white creatures occur once in every ten births. Also known as the Spirit Bear, they are given special significance by First Nations people. About 400 live in the area, most on Princess Royal Island.*

Above: Canoe paddles line a boat shed.
Opposite top right: There are no roads in Hartley Bay. Boardwalks, not sidewalks, connect the community.
Opposite bottom right: The view north up Grenville Channel off the bow of the SV Erramus.

Grenville Channel

"Last night a heavy fog came on, remaining with us the greater part of the way through the Grenville Canal, obscuring the land, which lay within a pistol-shot on either side. The heavy banks of fog mixing with the smoke of the funnel lay like bluffs of land ahead, and could be distinguished by a dark, gloomy outline, which might be fog or might be land. There was a tide running so that we could not stop, not go on, and there was never a sounding to be had." So wrote Molyneux St. John, a reporter for the Toronto Globe, describing a trip through Grenville Channel in 1876.

Grenville Channel's width of 0.3 km (0.2 mi) in places makes it one of the narrowest waterways used by large vessels on the Inside Passage. Its 45-mi (72 km) long steep sides are cut by spectacular waterfalls and the occasional entrance to quiet lagoons and anchorages. Lowe Inlet, one such refuge, is a traditional fishing ground of the Tsimshian Nation. BC's mainland coast is on the east side of Grenville Channel with Pitt Island to the west.

On July 6, 1793, a survey party from Captain George Vancouver's ship entered Grenville Channel. Captain Vancouver recorded the following: "At the south east point of entrance into this arm, which lies west about two miles from the rendezvous point, and for two miles within, the sea abounded with sea otters. These, in the most sportive manner, played about the boat, rearing themselves half way out of the water and holding up their young ones in the fore paws, as if to view the boats as they passed." ∎

How to Cook Prawns

"You know what to do with 'em?" asked the fisherman, after handing over a bag of fresh, squirming prawns at the Lund fuel barge one hot summer day.

Up until that moment, our closest relationship with a prawn had been while sitting at a linen covered table in a restaurant. "Nope," we said.

"First you clean 'em," he said. "Pull off the heads and toss those back in the chuck. Then, you find the biggest pot you got, fill it with water and add a whole bunch of salt. Then add some more. You bring the water to a boil, then drop in the prawns. As soon as they float, you scoop them out of the pot and put them into ice cold water.

"You got to do it right away," he emphasized, "or they get too tough. And that's it. Put 'em in a pan with a little oil, garlic, lemon juice, wine, and you got yourself a feed."

We thanked him and he hopped back aboard his vessel. He reminded us once again, "Lots of salt. Can't put in too much salt. It's strange, but it brings out the sweetness." Then he opened the throttle and chugged away from the dock.

A couple of hours later, at anchor in Squirrel Cove, we toasted the sunset and tested his advice. It was all good.

Above: *The sea is bountiful along the Inside Passage: salmon, cod, crab, halibut and prawns are among the seafood safely available. A member of the shrimp family (Pandalidae), prawns (Panndalus platyecros) are plentiful and easy to catch with the right equipment — a prawn trap, at least 400 feet of line, bait, and a float. Success is almost guaranteed if you go deep enough (at least 300 feet) and find the right spot — the mouth of an inlet is ideal. The authors caught this dinner at the mouth of Kumealon Inlet on Grenville Channel.*

Floyd Dundas,
Carpenter, Hartley Bay, BC

It's raining in the Gitga'at First Nations village of Hartley Bay. "What do you expect — it's a rain forest," one young resident dryly points out as he strolls along the boardwalk one early June morning.

Behind him an impressive half-finished long house sits patiently waiting for work to resume. Normally the construction site would be a hive of activity, but on this day, Floyd Dundas is the only one around.

"We're waiting for the supply barge," he explains. One of the problems of living in this remote Tsimshian community just off the south end of Grenville Channel is that there are no roads in or out. The village "streets" are boardwalks, charming to an outsider and practical given the climate; but no roads means it can take a long time to get materials. "The barge won't be here for another week and there's nothing for the others to do until it gets here with the windows," says Dundas. At least the roof is done and the walls are up, though, so he's protected from the rain. And he doesn't mind taking a few minutes to show visitors around the traditional building.

Almost all of the building is made from cedar, logged and milled in Hartley Bay. Some of the boards are 20 inches wide, 2 inches thick and 20 to 30 feet long — beautiful wood that would turn big city architects green with envy.

Obviously proud of the building, Dundas points out unique features like the traditional firepit — on the second floor. He gestures to massive glue-lam beams, several feet thick, that the roof rests on, ample protection from winter snow. He explains how he uses a power saw to cut miters in boards. The work is labour intensive, but they've got no shortage of labour in Hartley Bay.

"I used to be a fisherman," he

Left: *Hartley Bay bridge*
Right: *Floyd Dundas in the Hartley Bay big house he helped build.*

explains. "But I've always worked with wood, ever since I was a kid. When the fishing crapped out, I started doing carpentry full time."

Like many coastal communities, Hartley Bay once had a much larger fishing fleet than it does now. "We used to have 30 boats working out of here," he says. "Now it's down to two. It's been a big problem for us." There's never been any logging here — fishing was always the traditional source of income for the community.

The village is aware of the problems that such isolation and lack of employment can create for young people. A few years ago, residents voted to become "a dry village", which means liquor can't be sold or consumed in town. The policy was decided on by a vote of residents. "It surprised the non-drinkers," Dundas recalls, "because about 80 percent of the people were drinkers. But they voted for a dry village anyway — to protect our kids." The policy isn't rigidly enforced, but the boundaries are clear. "If I was caught drinking,

I'd lose my job and get a big fine," Dundas says.

And he doesn't want to lose his job. You get the feeling that it's not just the money. This man is proud of what he's helping to create for his community. "The beams and glue lams will be covered by totem poles and logs," Dundas says. He shows us where the large windows will go, looking out over Douglas Channel. On a clear day you might be able to see across to Princess Royal Island, the home of the mythical Kermode bear. The Gitga'at First Nation has about 640 hectares of reserve land, and a chunk of it is on Princess Royal Island.

Despite the fact that work is hard to come by, Dundas doesn't want to live anywhere else. "I worked in Rupert for a few years," he says, "but this is home." He heads back to the cedar planks and his careful cutting of mitered edges, doing what he can until the supply ship comes.

Previous page: Bear and salmon are two important species that help maintain the health of many Inside Passage ecosystems. Bears gather at streams and rivers as the fish migrate home to spawn and carry salmon carcass inland, which enriches soils and provides food for other species.

Above: Some of Prince Rupert's 780 commercial fishing vessels at dock in their home harbour. Two of North America's most productive salmon rivers, the Skeena and Nass, drain into Chatham Sound, just east of Prince Rupert. The area supports 11 processing plants.

Opposite top: Crab pots stacked by Prince Rupert's harbour

Opposite bottom left: This abandoned federal marine station, built in 1912, is in Casey Cove on Digby Island south of Prince Rupert. The five-acre site once featured an 800-ft seawall, a large superintendent's residence, staff quarters, a mess house, office buildings and several workshops. It is now private property.

Opposite bottom right: First Nations dancers join in Rupert's annual Seafest parade. The Tsimshian are the indigenous First Nations people in the area. Others include Haida, Gitksan and Nisga'a.

Prince Rupert

Besides being the last town in BC on the Inside Passage route north, Prince Rupert (pop. 16,700) is the third deepest natural harbour in the world. Rupert, as it is known locally, is also an important commercial fishery centre: it is home to the largest salmon cannery in the world and the oldest surviving cannery in the province. The Skeena River, second only to the Fraser River in its capacity to produce sockeye, hosts over five million spawning salmon a year and has one of the largest runs of wild steelhead in the world. Its estuary is an important ecosystem, hosting thousands of migratory birds each year.

Actually closer to Japan than Vancouver, the town was BC's first planned community, incorporated in 1910 as the terminus of the Grand Trunk Railway. Prince Rupert, the man, was first governor of the Hudson's Bay Company in 1670. The area was inhabited by Tsimshian First Nations people. Several petroglyphs in the area, including the impressive Man Who Fell From the Sky, attest to these earliest residents.

Many feel that Prince Rupert is synonymous with rain, and, with an average annual rainfall of 93 in (236 cm), about twice that of "rainy" Vancouver, the reputation is earned. Officially Canada's cloudiest place, the city enjoys about 6123 overcast hours each year. In October 1995, residents were deluged with 14 cm (5.5 in) of rain in one day, the greatest amount recorded in a 24-hour period. ■

Father William Duncan and Metlakatla

After Europeans had established fur-trade relationships with the First Nations people living along the Inside Passage, Christian missionaries followed. History books are full of descriptions of their efforts to convert and "civilize" the Native people. Most attempts, along with the introduction of diseases like smallpox and alcoholism, almost destroyed Northwest Native cultures.

William Duncan, a leather merchant from England, who arrived at the Hudson's Bay Company post at Fort Simpson in 1857, was determined that his missionary work would not only teach Christian ways to the 2300 Tsimshian people who lived near the post, but also prepare them for the new society into which they had been thrust.

Teaching himself to speak Tsimshian, he began preaching, but soon realized his efforts were having little effect. In an inspired move that meant his followers escaped the smallpox epidemic that soon swept through Fort Simpson, he decided to establish a utopian community away from the negative influence of the fur-trading culture (and also what he determined to be negative influences of the Tsimshian culture).

In 1862 Duncan and 400 of his congregation moved to Metlakatla, an uninhabited Tsimshian village on the shores of Venn Passage. They built a model community, with identical individual houses for families and a monstrous gothic-style church, as well as various enterprises, like a sawmill, a cannery, newspaper, rope-making shop, and cooperative store, which rendered them almost self-sufficient. Traditional celebrations, such as potlatch, were forbidden, and Duncan introduced more "civilized" leisure pursuits, like the formation of a brass band. Soon the community grew to over 1200 residents and developed an international reputation as a model Christian village.

Without Duncan's determination and vision, Metlakatla would never have flourished. But his determination also led to its destruction. One of the Tsimshian traditions that Duncan was determine to eradicate was the practise of ceremonial cannibalism. He therefore decided that the Tsimshian should not take part in holy communion because it would encourage, rather than discourage, the practise. But those higher up the church hierarchy did not agree. Duncan refused to capitulate and in 1887, along with 850 followers, moved again, this time to Annette Island in Alaska, where they established New Metlakatla.

Some accounts say that this time the undertaking was successful; others say that Duncan's determination and unswayable vision led to discord. In any event, Duncan died in New Metlakatla in 1918. Both communities survive today.

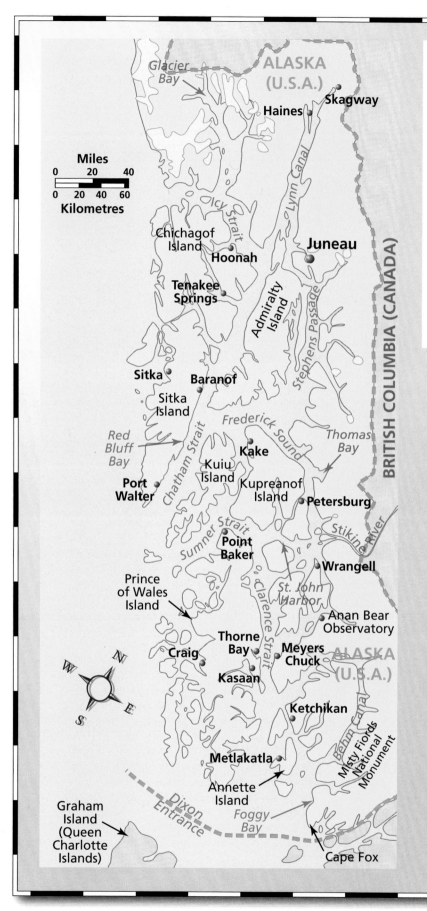

Map labels:

Glacier Bay

ALASKA (U.S.A.)

Skagway

Haines

Miles
0   20   40

Kilometres
0   20 40   60

Icy Strait

Lynn Canal

Chichagof Island

Juneau

Hoonah

Tenakee Springs

Admiralty Island

Stephens Passage

BRITISH COLUMBIA (CANADA)

Sitka

Baranof

Sitka Island

Red Bluff Bay

Chatham Strait

Frederick Sound

Thomas Bay

Kake

Kuiu Island

Kupreanof Island

Petersburg

Stikine River

Port Walter

Sumner Strait

Point Baker

Wrangell

Clarence Strait

St. John Harbor

Prince of Wales Island

Anan Bear Observatory

Thorne Bay

Meyers Chuck

ALASKA (U.S.A.)

Craig

Kasaan

Ketchikan

Behm Canal

Misty Fiords National Monument

Metlakatla

Annette Island

Dixon Entrance

Foggy Bay

Graham Island (Queen Charlotte Islands)

Cape Fox

W N E S

Alaska Facts Box

Total population: 626,932
Population density statewide:
  1 person per square mile
Motto: "North to the future"
Number of Glaciers: about 5000,
  the most in the world
Nickname: The Last Frontier
Bird: Willow ptarmigan
Fish: King salmon
Flower: Forget-me-not
Fossil: Woolly mammoth
Gem: Jade
Insect: Four-spot skimmer dragonfly
Sport: Dog mushing
Tree: Sitka spruce

Left: *Map illustrating the Inside Passage from Dixon Entrance to Skagway.*

SOUTHEAST: DIXON ENTRANCE TO SKAGWAY

Above: Lynn Canal, the end of the Inside Passage for Klondikers in the late 1890s.

The northernmost leg of the Inside Passage is through Alaska's Alexander Archipelago, a 450-km (280-mi) chain of over 1000 islands and countless mainland inlets and fjords known to locals as "Southeast". The U.S. Coast and Geodetic Survey named the archipelago in 1867 (the year Alaska was purchased from Russia), after Tsar Alexander II, Russia's ruler at the time. It also is known as the "Alaska Panhandle".

Eighty percent of Southeast Alaska is part of the 17-million-acre Tongass National Forest, the largest national forest in the United States. If you're outside a village or town, you're likely looking at it. Established in 1907, the Tongass is a multi-use forest, with 22 percent of the land currently eligible to be logged; other designated uses include public-use wilderness cabins, bear-viewing areas (the most popular being Anan Bear Observatory near Wrangell), and two national monuments — Admiralty Island and Misty Fjords.

The world's largest temperate rain forest, the Tongass has old-growth trees from 200 to 700 years old, and it contains the largest tracts of virgin old-growth trees left in America.

Southeast also has over 24,140 km (15,000 mi) of shoreline, 12 national wilderness areas, 15,000 bald eagles, 25,000 brown bears, 60 major glaciers, 33 communities and 70,000 residents. Besides eagles and bears, wildlife species include: humpback, orca, gray and minke whales; porpoises, dolphins, seals, and sea lions; salmon, halibut, crab and herring; puffins, hummingbirds, blue jays and auklets; wolves, mountain goats,

elk and moose; ice worms and banana slugs. More deer live in Southeast Alaska than people.

Three major ice fields are located here: the 3885 sq km (1,500 sq mi) Juneau Ice Field; the slightly smaller Stikine Ice Field near the communities of Wrangell and Petersburg; and the world famous Brady Ice Field in Glacier Bay National Park.

Weather is affected by the moisture that sweeps in from the Gulf of Alaska, and although many hear "Alaska" and think cold, snow and ice, the climate varies. Southeast tends to be milder than many people realize. The record for average rainfall is held by Little Port Walter, at the southern end of Baranof Island, with 559 cm (220 in). The record for rainfall in one day is held by Angoon on Admiralty Island, which received 39 cm (15.2 in) in 24 hours in October 1982. Skagway, on the other hand receives an annual rainfall of just 74 cm (29 in). And Kake boasts of its location in "the banana belt" — the low profile of the surrounding landscape results in relatively dry, mild weather.

Native American culture in Southeast is centered in Craig, Klawok, Hoonah, Hydaburg and Metlakatla. The major language groups are Tlingit, Tsimshian and Haida. About 20 percent of the population is Native American.

In 1963, the state of Alaska designated a water route called the Marine Highway that is serviced by state-run ferries. Currently nine ferries make scheduled visits to 32 Pacific ports from Bellingham, WA, to Dutch Harbour and Unalaska in the

Above: Advection fog is common in the southern reaches of Revillagigedo Channel. Foggy Bay provides a welcome sheltered harbour when visibility gets poor or strong southeasterlies blow up from Dixon Entrance. Right: The Tlingit village of Hoonah on Icy Strait operates under the native-run Sealaska Corporation.

Aleutian Islands, including many stops along the Inside Passage.

The Inside Passage route becomes less clear here, as several waterways allow protected passage north to Skagway or northwest to the Gulf of Alaska. Most cruise ships stop at Ketchikan, but from there smaller vessels, including the Alaska State Ferries, head north through Wrangell Narrows between Kupreanof and Mitkof islands, while larger vessels choose the wider Chatham Strait between Kuiu and Baranof islands to the west. ■

Revillagigedo Channel

This wide 40-nautical-mile-long channel, the most southern part of Alaska's Inside Passage, extends from Dixon Entrance to Tongass Narrows and Clarence Strait. The name is pronounced ruh-vee-uh-guh-GAY-doh, but locals shorten it to Revilla. It's a joining together of one of the names of Don Juan Vincente de Guemes Pacheco de Padilla Horcasitas, Count of Revilla Gigedo. Sr. Vincente, the Viceroy of Mexico, has a nearby island named after him as well: 90-km- (55-mi-) long Revillagigedo Island at the north of the channel, where the city of Ketchikan is located.

Much of the west shoreline of the channel is part of Annette Island. A Canadian Air Force base during World War II, Annette Island is also the site of Alaska's first and only Indian reservation, established in 1891 for Tsimshian people who moved here from BC with Father William Duncan to set up a model Christian community in 1887 (see Metlakatla, pg. 99). Unlike other Native Americans in Alaska, Metlakatla tribal leaders opted out of a statewide settlement in favour of keeping their reservation status.

The 86,000-acre reservation and surrounding 915 m (3,000 ft) of coastal waters are controlled by the community, not the state. The Tsimshian oversee commercial fishing in the area as well as their own tribal court system. ■

Sea Otter
(Enhydra lutris)

The soft fur of the sea otter, the thickest of any mammal, became highly prized in the early fur trade (see pg. 104), particularly in Chinese markets: at the height of the market, one pelt could fetch as much as $1000. With a luxurious 850,000 to one million hairs per square inch, the sea otter became highly prized and intensely hunted.

Once ranging from Alaska to Mexico, they are the only mammals, other than primates, that use tools to feed, breaking open the shells of clams and abalone with stones. When underwater searching for food, they store their catch in loose skin folds at their armpits — a necessity given that adult sea otters can eat 25 to 30 percent of their body weight in one day.

Almost rendered extinct by 1812, it took almost 100 years before an international treaty banned the killing of sea otters (in 1911). Their numbers gradually increased during the 20th century, and now they inhabit coastal kelp beds from Alaska to California. (The kelp acts as an anchor that the sea otters use to wrap themselves in when they are resting.)

A 1995 estimate put the population at about 1,500 in BC and over 150,000 in Alaska. Considered an endangered species, the sea otter has been protected by law since 1970.

Right: A female sea otter holding her pup on her chest.

LANDING A CARGO OF FURS   PRINCE RUPERT B.C.

Early Fur Trading

When Russian explorers Vitus Bering and Aleksi Cherikov crossed the Gulf of Alaska and first sighted land in 1741, they began a marine fur trade route that stretched as far south as California and opened up Southeast Alaska to European settlement.

Looking for a fur supply for Chinese markets, the Russians found a seemingly endless supply of sea otters as well as seals and other mammals. Although the Russian government was not primarily interested in settlement, by 1799 the trade had become so profitable that Grigorii Shelikhov petitioned the government for exclusive rights, and in 1799, the Russian American Company was created. Aleksandr Baranof subsequently established a Russian trading base at Sitka — and a firm Russian presence in Southeast Alaska. The Russian American Company became the governing power in Alaska until 1867.

News of the Russian trade attracted Spanish and then British explorers. After reading James Cook's accounts of his 1778 explorations of the Alaska coast, Captain James Hanna arrived on the *Sea Otter* in 1785, trading furs in Nootka Sound that fetched over $20,000 in Canton. American Robert Gray joined the hunt in 1789, and within a year American traders, mainly from Boston, dominated. Between 1790 and 1812 as many as two dozen vessels traded on the coast, almost totally eradicating the sea otter population in their harvest of furs.

The fur traders supplied the coastal First Nations people with their first contact with Europeans. The Natives became involved in the fur trade, which radically changed their traditional ways forever. By the time Alexander Mackenzie arrived at Bella Coola in 1793, trading between Native people and Europeans along the coast was common.

By the 1820s the glory days of the sea otter fur trade were in decline. The Hudson's Bay Company took over from American traders, establishing forts on the coast (like Fort McLoughlin at Bella Bella and Fort Wrangell in Southeast) for its land-based fur trading empire.

The decline of the fur trade set the stage for the Russians to sell Alaska to the United States in 1867 for $USD 7.2 million. Since fur resources were depleted, the two-cents-an-acre purchase became known as "Seward's Folly", after US Secretary of State William Seward who arranged the deal.

Seals and other fur-bearing animals continued to supply the fur trade however, and it remained important to the Alaska economy and many communities along the Northern Inside Passage until the late 19th and early 20th centuries.

Opposite: *"Landing a cargo of furs, Prince Rupert"*
ca 1910.
Top: *Tlingit seal hunters' beach camp, Glacier Bay,*
1899.
Bottom left: *Drawing of Russian American Company*
site in Sitka Sound in 1805.
Bottom right: *Seal skins drying, Alaska, 1899.*

George Porter,
Marine Pilot,
Ketchikan, Alaska

All I wanted when I retired," says Ketchikan resident George Porter, "was to be able to sum up my career with one word — 'uneventful.'"

"And he did," wife Gail proudly notes. "He's one of the few that can say that."

Most people might wish for notable events to mark a career, but not if you're in George Porter's line of work. Recently retired, George has been a marine pilot for almost 30 years. Altogether, he's spent 48 years at sea, starting with the US Coast Guard, which he joined in 1953.

Marine pilots work coastal areas, rivers and lakes around the world, guiding the movements of large vessels through unfamiliar local waters. Southeast Alaska marine pilots' territory is from Dixon Entrance to Yakutat on the Gulf of Alaska. "He has to know every rock," says Gail.

Most cruise ship passengers don't even know he's aboard. Pilots usually arrive at a ship by powerboat (sometimes by helicopter), clamber aboard, stay with the ship while it is in the designated territory, and then leave by the same method. His average stay is about four days.

He may be invisible, but he's certainly methodical. He does his homework, studying and updating charts, learning all he can about the vessel and captain, analyzing weather forecasts, tide and current tables, and assembling other information before he goes to work.

"It isn't anything you do piecemeal," says George. "It requires 24-hour-a-day concentration. Even when you're not on the ship, you're still preparing for the next one, or thinking about what you did on the last one. It takes a lot out of you."

On this pleasant July evening, he and Gail have just sailed across Dixon Entrance from their home in

Above: *George and Gail Porter on the* SV Marlyn *in Prince Rupert.*

Ketchikan to Prince Rupert on their 36-foot sailboat, the *Marlyn*. But over his career, he has advised captains aboard much larger and more complicated vessels: cargo ships, cruise ships, large yachts and even the USS *Ohio*, a Trident submarine. "That was the highlight," George chuckles. "I was like a kid in a candy store. I looked around at all those dials and screens and thought 'I don't know what's going on here, but I'm the pilot!' It was great!"

"He was up in that conning tower," prompts Gail, "which is what — 40? 60 feet up?"

"I don't know," says George, "but it's pretty small, and I'm standing there straddling this hatch, and I can look all the way down to the bottom of the sub. If you miss a step or slip, you're gone."

Falls and slips are a major occupational hazard. Boarding a cruise ship is relatively straightforward, but getting on a cargo ship can involve clambering 30 feet up a rope ladder, then transferring to an accommodation ladder, a total climb to the bridge of perhaps 100 feet. And all this with the tools-of-the-trade on your back: charts, notes, binoculars, dividers, VHF, and whatever else is useful. Some pilots even take their own electronic chartplotters. In a high sea, the risks are obvious.

One might expect a marriage might be at risk as well. But it doesn't

seem so with Gail and George Porter. "The wife of any seafarer raises the kids, pays the bills and manages life," she says philosophically. "In some cases he would bring a ship into Ketchikan, get off that ship, have me meet him there with a new suitcase of clothes and get back on another ship. It's gruelling."

It can also be lonely. Once the kids were grown, Gail bought a small flower business in Ketchikan, expanding it to two shops with 18 employees over the 20 years she ran it. "We were the first store in the mall," says George proudly.

Both retired now, George still spends a lot of time of the waters he navigated for so many years, but now Gail comes with him, cruising and fishing. And despite all the high tech bridges he's been on, his own vessel isn't equipped with a lot of new-fangled electronics. "If I can't get to Point A to Point B without that stuff," George says, "I'm going to quit.

"He's the last of the resistance," says Gail.

"Oh, we'll probably end up getting a GPS on the sailboat," George allows. "But don't tell any of my brother pilots."

He may be a purist, but it's worked well. "No collisions. No drownings," says George. No events.

≈Ketchikan

The first port of call for most Alaska-bound vessels is Ketchikan, Alaska's southernmost and fourth-largest city. Claiming to have the world's largest collection of totem poles, Ketchikan was originally a Tlingit fishing camp. The Native cultural influence is seen everywhere, with several totem parks in and around the city and Native motifs decorating many buildings. The name "Ketchikan" is derived from a Tlingit word meaning creek of "the thundering wings of an eagle".

Mining, logging and fishing were the area's economic mainstays once European settlement began in the 1880s with the establishment of a cannery, but since the 1980s tourism has become increasingly important. Ketchikan is a major stop for cruise ships, with many downtown shops only open when the cruise ships come in during the summer season.

The town bills itself as the Salmon Capitol of the World, and given that anglers catch spawning fish off the main bridge right downtown before the fish head up Ketchikan Creek, it seems a righteous claim. At one time Ketchikan supported over a dozen canneries: today there are four fishery plants, but sport fishing is a popular pastime. The boat basin, also at the mouth of the creek, used to be the baseball diamond — when the tide was out.

Ketchikan is visually charming, with much of the town hanging on stilts drilled into Tongass Narrows or clinging to the edge of the mountain. The views can be spectacular — when you can see them — the town averages 4 m (13 ft) of rain annually. ■

Left: Cruise ships are a common sight in downtown Ketchikan during the summer. In 2001, cruise ships tied up to the docks 470 times, bringing 652,486 passengers to the city. Ketchikan has a population of 7,922.
Right: One of the most photographed places in Southeast Alaska is Ketchikan's historic Creek Street, where brothels operated until the 1970s.
Previous pages: Kwakwaka'wakw dugout canoes under sail in 1914. So sturdy were these vessels that famous sailor John Voss used a dugout canoe, the Tilikum, when he set off from Victoria on his around-the-world voyage in 1901.

Clarence Strait

Stretching 112 nautical miles from Dixon Entrance in the south to Sumner Strait in the north, Clarence Strait is a major thoroughfare on Southeast's marine highway. The strait divides south of Zarembo Island: to the northwest is picturesque Snow Passage and to the northeast Stikine Strait heads to Wrangell, both connecting to Sumner Strait.

The west side of the Passage is bounded by Prince of Wales Island, the third largest island in the US. (Hawaii and Kodiak Island are the top two.) Mostly national forest, the 5778 sq km (2231 sq mi) island is largely uninhabited, with Klawock on the west coast housing the state's first cannery in 1878. Other towns include Craig, Hydaburg, Kasaan and Thorne Bay.

Most towns and cities in Southeast are waterbound;

Terri Metcalf,
Jill of All Trades, Port Protection

As a single woman living in a remote area of Southeast, Terri Metcalf is necessarily a "Jill of All Trades". She also seems an embodiment of the independent Alaskan spirit. "I'm always saying, 'Yeah, sure, I'll do it!' before I know what I'm getting myself into," says the 40-something wonder woman. She's an artist, set builder, prospector, commercial fisher, research coordinator, and has guided a BBC crew wanting to film a story about nearby On Your Knees Cave, a recently discovered archeological site. Right now she's building a restaurant in Port Protection, "with a dance floor." Raised in Ketchikan, she spent time in "the lower forty-eight" searching for home before she returned to Alaska and discovered it at the tip of Prince of Wales Island. "I needed to get happy," she says of her journey. "I discovered I needed to be around the water or be near water people. Folks who live on an island have to live with themselves. The people here are a different breed. They're the ones who go past the end of the road."

Above: *Terri Metcalf about to guide visiting scientists to Sumner Strait kelp beds.*

Caves and Karst

Much of the Alexander Archipelago is karst: limestone and marble riddled with caves, sinkholes, pits, underground streams, springs and grikes (vertical, trenchlike cracks in bedrock that channel water downward). One section of Prince of Wales Island is estimated to contain more than 10,000 sinkholes per square mile — some several metres across, others invisible. Hundreds of caves have been located across this region, with dozens of new ones found each year. Estimates of undiscovered, "significant" caves run into the thousands.

In 1990, the first vertebrate fossils were found, and a major research effort began to explore this new scientific resource. Geologists and spelunkers have mapped miles of caves, which have formed over thousands of years. One impressive karst feature discovered in the Tongass is the El Capitan cave on the northwestern side of Prince of Wales Island, which has more than three km (two mi) of underground passageways. Nearby is El Cap Pit with a vertical drop of 182 m (598 feet) — the deepest vertical shaft in the United States.

The caves are also important from an archaeological standpoint. Explorers have found cave paintings made by people who lived thousands of years ago, and a human jaw bone recovered from a Prince of Wales cave has been radio-carbon dated at 9,730 years, the oldest human

Above: *Explorers in an inflatable investigate the mouth of a large sea cave.*

remains found in Alaska. The caves have yielded ancient animal fragments as well: bear bones dating back 30,000 to 40,000 years, and a 45,000-year-old marmot tooth.

Perhaps the most significant aspect of the Tongass karst is environmental. For reasons not fully understood, trees tend to grow bigger on karst and salmon streams in karstlands host huge runs of fish — up to 10 times more than in non-karst areas. Predictably, the debate between foresters, scientists, cave experts and environmentalists on how to manage Alaska's karstlands is ongoing.

Haines, Skagway and Hyder (on Portland Canal) are the only three that connect to the outside world by road. Some, like Juneau, Ketchikan, Petersburg and Wrangell, have extensive road systems that may go well beyond the city limits. But others are roadless — tiny places where neighbours visit over pathways or by boat, and the only motorized vehicles are ATVs or golf carts. Roadless communities can be found all along the Inside Passage from BC's Desolation Sound north, Southeast's seem particularly remote. Clarence Strait, Prince of Wales Island and Chatham Strait (further north) host several of these communities in Southeast. Their often very isolated locations and hardy, independent residents seem to provide a glimpse into the heart and soul of Alaska. ■

Sumner Strait

Sumner Strait is a wide, major inlet stretching 80 nautical miles from the Gulf of Alaska east to the mainland at the mouth of the Stikine River. On the northern side it is bordered by Kuiu, Kupreanof and Mitkof islands. Its southern boundary edges the northwest and northern shores of Prince of Wales, Zarembo, and Wrangell islands.

There is very little settlement in this area, with Wrangell at the eastern end of the strait and the roadless fishing communities of Port Protection and Port Baker at the northern tip of Prince of Wales Island among the few settlements.

It was near these latter communities that members of a logging survey crew came across On Your Knees Cave in 1993.

Above: Clarence Strait where it meets Behm Canal north of Ketchikan.
Following page left: Kasaan, a Haida settlement on Prince of Wales Island dating back to the 1700s, was originally Tlingit territory. The site of a copper mining camp in the 1890s and a cannery between 1902 and 1953, the old village burned in 1918.
Following page right: A foggy morning at St. John Harbour, off Sumner Strait.

About one km from the ocean and 125 m above sea level, the cave contained bone fragments of a grizzly bear reported to be 41,600 radiocarbon years old, human remains dated at 9880 years and a bone tool dated at 10,300 years old. It is considered to be the most significant archeological and paleontological site in Southeast Alaska.

Most of the larger cruise ships leaving Ketchikan will travel north up Clarence Strait through Snow Passage to Sumner Strait, then around Cape Decision and north to Chatham Strait. But smaller vessels often choose a stricter interpretation of the "Inside" Passage, heading north from Sumner Strait through picturesque but shallow Wrangell Narrows.

When the immense tidal currents of Sumner Strait meet with strong ocean winds, very violent sea conditions can occur. At other times, the strait is benign and pleasant, a boon to logging barges, fishing vessels, and pleasure boaters. ■

Crabs

Thirty-five species of crab are found in Inside Passage waters, falling into three main groups: Brachyurnas, lithodid, and hermit. "True" crabs (Brachyurans), including spider crabs, Dungeness and red rocks, have four pairs of walking legs plus claws. The lithodid crabs, which appear to have only three pairs of walking legs, include king crabs and box crabs. Hermit crabs are sometimes hairy in appearance with long antennae and usually have one claw larger than the other. With soft, unprotected abdomens they like to use empty snail shells as shelter.

Above: A Dungeness on the way to market.

Crabs crawl along the sea bottom eating algae, small marine animals and detritus. Periodically, they shed their exoskeletons, go into hiding as they grow larger and form new shells, and emerge when the shell has hardened. Crabs are also able to regenerate limbs and pincers that have been torn or lost.

The four most often found on dinner tables are Dungeness, red rock, spider and Alaska king.

Native American Land Claims in Southeast

Unlike in BC and Washington, federal Indian reservations are not the norm in Alaska. The federal Alaska Native Claims Settlement Act (ANCSA), passed in 1971, established 12 regional Alaska Native corporations, giving them control of one-ninth of the state's land plus $962.5 million in compensation in exchange for dropping all claims to Alaska.

Headquartered in Juneau, the Sealaska Corporation oversees Southeast Alaska, in association with the Tlingit and Haida Central Council. With over 16,000 Alaska Native shareholders, Sealaska is the largest private landowner in Southeast. Principal investments are in forest products, financial markets, telecommunications, entertainment, plastics, and mineral exploration and development.

Natives and non-natives in and outside of Alaska are still evaluating ANCSA and its effects. While many support Native corporations, critics' fears include the possibility that Native corporations could become conduits for larger multi-national interests.

Steve Peavey & Cassy Peavey,
Meyers Chuck, Alaska

Left: *Cassy and Steve Peavey, Meyers Chuck.*
Right: *Dock, Meyers Chuck. Settlers began living here in the late 1800s and a cannery was established in 1916.*

Steve and Cassy Peavey have lived in the tiny roadless community of Meyer's Chuck since 1960. That's not counting the eight years Steve lived here with his parents when his father was discharged from the Marine Corps in the mid-1940s. He and Cassy met when his folks moved across Clarence Strait to the village of Kasaan. She was 10; he was 15. They married when she was 16 and moved back to Meyers Chuck the next year.

They logged. They fished. They raised two sons. And they worked together to build up their homestead. "What it is," says Cassy, looking back on their years together, "is a whole lifetime. That's what it is."

Nowadays, only 10 people live in Meyer's Chuck year round, about 30 or so in the summers. "During its heyday," recalls Steve, "there were probably 60 people living here. Of course, we didn't know it was the heyday," he adds. "This place is dying. It really is." Cassy doesn't like hearing him say that, although she almost admits its true. "It's just such a nice place," she says with a sad smile. "But you can't make a living anymore," says Steve.

He retired from fishing a few years ago, although he still keeps his well-maintained vessel at the public dock across the small bay from his house. Cassy used to fish with him, although she never liked it much. "I used to get seasick," she confesses, "but he was away so much it was the only way I could see him."

It's not an easy place to live. There are no roads in or out. The mail plane brings the groceries. There's no public electricity. If you want power, you generate your own. Just like if you want heat in the winter, you put up your own firewood.

And the weather presents its own challenges. "It can get pretty ugly out there [in Chatham Strait]," Cassy acknowledges. "In the winter, sometimes the wind can get up to 100 miles an hour; it's common for it to be blowing 70. When it's like that, you can't even go down on the dock."

But at the same time, it is peaceful, they agree. Herons occasionally watch for fish on their dock. The tides rise and fall with dependable regularity. Eagles soar overhead.

Cassy has spent the last few

winters focussing her creative talents on new forms. "I've always been an artist," she admits, with a slow smile, "but now it's a hobby that earns money." She began with cedar coffee tables for her sons one Christmas. Then she tried her hand at smaller items — boxes, masks, animal carvings and even halibut hooks.

She's taken a couple of courses from master carvers in Southeast, but she's had no formal training. "I've always been one of these people who said 'Okay we need a cupboard, so I'll build a cupboard.'" No need to deal with the hassle of shipping things to galleries in Ketchikan or Juneau, either. She sells everything she makes at the artist-run gallery right in Meyers Chuck. But she's one of the lucky ones.

"The future looks a little grim," says Steve. "No one's moving in. And you want someone you can argue with." He peers out the window of his living room across to the community dock. "I like to yell at the tourists when they tie up in the middle of the dock. We watched you last night when you came in," he says with a grin. "Luckily you did okay, but I was ready to let you have it."

Kelp

Kelp is large, brown seaweed or algae that grows underwater and on rocky shores in cold waters throughout the world. Kelps vary in size and form, and include true kelp (belonging to the Order Laminariales), giant kelp and bladder kelp.

They do not have roots, but cling to rocks with grippers called holdfasts, which are strong enough to take the battering of even the fiercest storms. From these holdfasts grows a slender stalk with long, leaf-like blades.

Southeastern Alaska is home to kelp forests of split kelp *(Laminaria bongardiana)*, bull kelp *(Nereocystis luetkeana)*, brown algae *(Alaria fistulosa* and *Agarum cribrosum)*, and ribbon or wing kelp *(Alaria crispa)*. The abundant bull kelp usually grows 11 metres long (30 to 35 ft), but have been found up to 39 metres (118 ft) in length, with blades alone measuring up to 11 meters (33 feet). The bull kelp has a long, hollow stem attached to a bulb or bladder called a pneumatocyst, which acts as a float, keeping the blades up near the sunlight and the plant sitting vertically in the water.

This plant has a one-year life cycle. Microscopic spores emitted in the fall live through the winter to produce new kelp each spring. During the warm months, the plant grows rapidly, forming its sturdy stem. In the winter, kelp plants die and large accumulations wash onto

Above: *Detail of kelp and seaweed at Codville Lagoon, BC.*

area beaches. Harvested kelps yield algin, a substance that is used in the manufacture of ice cream, salad dressing, beer, paper, cosmetics, fertilizer, animal feed and many other products.

Chris Dahl
Entrepreneur, Point Baker

The skiff winds through a narrow channel filled with dark brown gleaming kelp fronds. The deep blue-green water lies clear between the long wavy strands of kelp, multi-armed starfish and white outer-space anemones. The scene looks like something from a George Lucas sci-fi drawing board, but these are the waters of Point Baker, at the northwest tip of Prince of Wales Island.

The kelp, a nuisance to boaters, is the stuff of Chris Dahl's dreams. A former fisherman, the Washington native has for the past six years been building a kelp harvesting business in this tiny community. "We're the only company in Alaska making kelp products," he says.

He first came to Alaska when he was a teenager — "on vacation with my father in a 50 foot Chris Craft. I took one look at the place and said, 'I'm home.'" He settled here 25 years ago and fished for a living. But when the fishery began declining, Dahl looked around to see what else he could do. His gaze landed on kelp.

A half dozen people work for Dahl, harvesting the long brown fronds just across Sumner Strait in Rocky Bay. They pull in 50,000 pounds a year, working two or three days a week during the season. Harvesters locate a patch of kelp, then gather it to the boat, cutting the fronds into lengths as they pull it aboard, leaving the "hold fast" to grow another frond. "It's really physical work," Dahl admits. "But if they work hard, they can make about $300 in a half day." That may sound like a lot of money, but the season is short, and Dahl's facility has a limited capacity. And kelp grows in rocky areas close to shore, which can also make harvesting dangerous. "But if the weather turns bad, I'll yank them," he says. "No one's going to die harvesting kelp off of my boat."

Left: *Bull kelp floating in Point Baker.*
Right: *Chris Dahl surrounded by barrels of kelp slurry ready for shipping.*

Dahl describes his small plant as "a work in progress". A few metres from his house, a series of small platforms and sheds in varying stages of completion are the heart of the business. Upstairs in the office, above a half finished space that will house more processing operations but now serves as a temporary bunk house, two scientists from San Diego are getting ready for the day's work. Chris Dahl's low key operation has suddenly attracted the attention of NASA. The San Diego scientists are using a high-tech digital imaging system to photograph Alaska KelpCo's harvest area from the air. Their results, along with other documentation by a team from the University of Alaska, will help create a sustainable harvesting plan — and permanent licensing, which will make KelpCo a more attractive investment opportunity. And it looks like what's good for KelpCo will be good for Point Baker. A solid kelp harvesting business will mean jobs for at least some of the town's 40 or so residents. And with the price of fish at an all time low, that has to be a welcome development. Almost everyone who lives here has come from someplace else, and could move on, but a local economy would provide work opportunities close to home.

Dahl gestures to a window in the cabin he shares with his wife and son that looks over a tiny bay and on into Sumner Strait. "We look out here and see whales breaching," he says. "Every day there's a whale here. We leave our window open at night and we can hear them sleeping." He imitates a low rumbling sound. He says it again, marvelling. "Every day there's a whale here." You get the sense that Chris Dahl is definitely home.

Above: The paddlewheeler SS Port Simpson *on the Stikine River in the early 1900s. These vessels provided an important transportation service until the 1970s.*
Page 114 left: Point Baker, on the northern tip of Prince of Wales Island, has a population of about 40 permanent residents. Traditionally a fishing community, fish buyers set up stations here in the 1930s and homesteaders followed.
Page 114 right: The old general store in Meyers Chuck. In 1939, 107 residents lived full-time in the town, supporting a post office, store, barber shop, bakery, bar, and machine shop.

≈Stikine River

Meaning "Great River" in Tlingit, the Stikine, with a watershed area encompassing nearly 50,000 sq km (20,000 sq mi), is one of the three major river systems on the Inside Passage. Although most of the river's 640 km (1030 mi) is in British Columbia, it meets the sea in Alaska just north of Wrangell — the north arm into the eastern end of Frederick Sound and the south arm at the eastern end of Sumner Strait. The passage of water between these two arms is known as Dry Strait. Although the delta is too shallow for much marine traffic, it is a major salmon spawning area and home to many species of wildlife.

With an average flow of 740 cubic metres (968 cu yd) per second, the Stikine is considered one of the top whitewater rafting rivers in the world. However, on its route to the sea, it passes through BC's version of the Grand Canyon, a 100-km-long (62-mi), 330-metre (1083 ft) deep channel that even the most expert whitewater enthusiasts won't challenge.

The Stikine has had enormous significance to the people of this area. For both First Nations and subsequent residents it was an important transportation route. The Tlingit maintained an active trading economy with the upstream Tahltan Nation, using the river as their highway. After European fur traders made first contact in 1838, the Hudson's Bay Company established several fur trading posts along its banks. When, starting in the 1850s, miners made several gold strikes along the Stikine and in the Atlin, Cassiar, Liard and Klondike regions, the Stikine became an important transportation route to the goldfields. In the late 1800s, paddlewheelers travelled the river between Wrangell and Telegraph Creek, which became the first leg of the "all-Canadian route" to the Yukon during the Klondike Gold Rush — a service that continued until the 1970s. Today several adventure tour companies offer trips up the Stikine along the same route.

The BC government declared the Stikine a heritage river in 1995. ■

≈Wrangell

The only city in Alaska to have existed under four nations and three flags (Stikine Tlingit, Russia, Great Britain and USA), Wrangell is a very friendly town. Its 2550 residents may be island bound, but they don't seem to mind; they greet you on the street, offer directions to strangers, and invite you into their homes.

At the north end of Wrangell Island, this area was fished and hunted by Tlingit people before the Russians erected Fort Redoubt St. Dionysius in 1834. Six years later, the Hudson's Bay Company ran it as Fort Stikine. After American occupation in 1867, the town was named Fort Wrangell, after Russian admiral Baron Ferdinand Petrovich von Wrangell, the sixth Chief Manager of the Russian American Company from 1830 to 1835.

Like many settlements along the Inside Passage, Wrangell's fortunes have been closely linked to mining, fishing and logging and now tourism. The Stikine River, which empties into Sumner Strait just 10 km (6 mi) north of Wrangell, has played an important part in the town's development. In 1872, the Stikine became an important transportation route for miners rushing to BC's Cassiar goldfields (until the strike played out a decade later). In 1887, a cannery opened that processed Stikine salmon, followed by a mill to build packing boxes.

Today Wrangell is visited by smaller cruise ships and the Alaska state ferries. It is a popular centre for outdoor recreation with the Stikine River, Anan Bear Reserve and Le Conte Glacier part of the attraction. ■

Above: *Looking across Sumner Strait to the Coast Range on the mainland at Petroglyph Beach. A state historic site, the beach holds dozens of petroglyphs carved in rocks that are covered at high tide.*

Frederick Sound

This wide 100-nautical-mile passageway connects with Chatham Strait on the west and Stephens Passage in the northeast arching and narrowing as it heads southeast to Dry Strait and the Stikine River estuary. Icebergs from North America's southernmost active tidal glacier, Le Conte Glacier, often calve into the eastern arm of Frederick Sound. The glacier startled those who watch these things by waking up from a 32-year sleep in 1995. That year it retreated, suddenly dropping a kilometre (.5 mi) of ice into the water.

Frederick Sound is also a common feeding ground for humpback whales during the summer months: some say it is the prime humpback-viewing area on the Inside Passage. Making up for a long winter fast in the tropics where the females give birth, here hundreds of them fill up on krill and herring. Among humpbacks' more fascinating pursuits are the males' singing (which they do in their southern migration), cooperative "bubble" feeding and breaching, where they leap completely out of the water — 40 tonnes of cetacean glory. ■

Top left: *The MV Spirit of 98, a small Seattle-based cruise ship, enters Wrangell Narrows at Petersburg. Prominent in the mountains behind is 2767-m (9077-ft) Devil's Thumb, one of the few named peaks in the icefields.*
Top right: *Chief Shakes tribal house in Wrangell, built in 1940 when the last Chief Shakes was named, is a replica*

of a high-caste Tlingit house. Several totems, carved in the 1930s, also are on the site.
Bottom: *Seal pups can often be seen floating on icebergs near Le Conte Glacier, off Frederick Sound's southeastern arm.*

Bald Eagle
(Haliaeetus leucocephalus)

Of all the wildlife species found along the Inside Passage, the eagle is one of the most identifiable. Golden eagles *(Aquila chrysaetos)* can be seen in the Puget Sound area and Fraser River lowlands, but it is the bald eagles, seen year round all the way from Seattle to Skagway, that seem synonymous with this part of the world.

Following herring runs in the spring and gathering around spawning salmon in the late summer and fall, bald eagles (from the Welsh word "balde" meaning "white") are found only in North America. They prefer to nest in tall old-growth trees, ideally Sitka spruce, with a view of the water. In Southeast there is one eagle nest for every 1.25 miles of shoreline, with Admiralty Island having the greatest density of nesting birds. The largest gathering of bald eagles in the world (about 3500) reportedly takes place at the Chilkat Bald Eagle Preserve near Haines during the late run of salmon from October to December.

There may be no more magnificent sight than a mature bald eagle gliding, swooping and diving against a backdrop of coastal wilderness, but it is a less-known fact that eagles also swim, using a kind of over-hand "butterfly"-stroke with their wings. They feed on fish, which they often pluck right out of the water, spying their prey from hundreds of metres high in the air and then diving straight down at speeds of up to 160 kph (100 mph). (Normal flight speed is about 50 to 60 kph — 30 to 40 mph). When food is scarce they will also feed on small mammals and shellfish. Eagles are classed as raptors and will often eat dead prey; biologists consider this "clean-up" behaviour an important contribution to the eco-system.

Bald eagles take about five years to mature, but when fully grown they measure about one metre in length, weighing 4 to 6 kg (8 to 14 lbs) with a wing span of over two metres (about seven to seven-and-a-half feet). Females are larger than males. They often return to the same nest for brooding, adding more and more twigs each year. The Endangered Animals Center reports one eagle nest, apparently used for 34 years, weighed over two tonnes.

Eagles are a very important symbol in First Nations art and mythology, respected for intelligence, power and extraordinary vision. The eagle clan or crest will most likely be the most powerful and respected in a hierarchy, and these attributes are reflected in their representation in mythology. The feathers are often used in rituals and are associated with healing powers; down is a symbol of peace and friendship. Eagle is often linked with Raven in myths and stories, particularly in the Haida traditions, where they are seen as two halves of the great whole.

The bald eagle has been the symbol of the USA since the Continental Congress declared it so in 1782. On the endangered species list in the US, eagles are protected by laws in Alaska that make it illegal to kill or possess an eagle, alive or dead or to possess any part of an eagle, including feathers.

Doug Brown,

Crab fisherman,
Garibaldi, Oregon

Left: *Doug Brown beside the* MV Kolchiss, *Wrangell.*
Right: *The* MV Kolchiss *crew prepare mink bait for their crab traps.*

On a sunny June day, Oregon-based Doug Brown is about to leave Wrangell for the opening of the Southeast Alaska crab fishery. The wharf and docks are abuzz with activity. Dozens of boats, stacked high with crab pots, wait in the harbour. Crew load supplies, bait traps, and make last-minute checks of equipment.

Brown expects it to be a competitive season. "The salmon industry is really on its lips because the price of salmon is so poor," says Brown, gesturing to several large purse seiners tied up at the end of the dock. "About half of that fleet lost their market this year," he says. As a result some of those fishermen bought crab permits from people who weren't working them much.

The crab fishery here is "limited entry" — only so many permits available and each permit with a specified number of pots. "They haven't actually increased the total

number of pots," Brown says, "But when you go out and spend 50,000 bucks for a permit, you're going to go fishing. So the same number of pots are going to be fished a lot harder."

It's competitive, but Brown says there are no real secrets in crabbing ("You need a muddy bottom, everybody knows that"), but you do need a little bit of savvy. "You can wander around out there forever and not catch anything," he says. "There are guys I've run into who could catch a salmon in a bathtub. And there are guys, if you put them in a hatchery pond with a thousand fish, they couldn't hook one in ten years."

You also need to work hard and efficiently. Brown, his partner, and their crew seem to have it down. "We lay out a string of pots," he explains, "each one with an individual buoy. When the pot comes up, the crew empty it, rebait it and about the time they're set, the boat's at the next

buoy. They kick the pot off, pick up the next buoy, put it in the block, and if you're good at it, you just keep going."

Sounds like it's not a bad life. Brown pays close attention to the weather and refuses to go out in dangerous conditions. He allows that in a good year, between fishing both here and Oregon, he can make a living in three or four months. And one thing crabbers don't have to worry about is over-fishing. "Although crabs are cyclical," Brown says, "it looks like it would be impossible to fish them out." The pots are constructed so sexually active males are usually too small to be trapped and it's illegal to keep females, so only the older males are harvested.

Ultimately, though, Brown says, "It's a crap shoot. We'll probably take about 20,000 to 50,000 pounds in ten or eleven days here. But you never know if it will be a good season."

≈Petersburg

The self-proclaimed "Halibut Capitol of the World", Petersburg, with a population of 3200, is the quintessential cannery town. Originally a Tlingit summer fish camp, the permanent settlement of Petersburg was founded by Norwegian-American Peter Buschmann who built a cannery and sawmill here in 1897. (Many of his fellow-Norwegians joined him and the town has a distinct Scandinavian ambience.) Buschmann packed his fish with ice from nearby Le Conte Glacier, Alaska's most southerly tidewater glacier and a big tourist attraction. Sandy Beach, just outside of town, is the site of 3000-year-old fish traps, which some experts believe are found nowhere else in the world.

The largest halibut fishery in the state is based in Petersburg, and during the summer, an international array of cannery workers come to process 51 million kg (113 million lbs) of fish and shellfish in the town's four plants.

Petersburg is at the northern end of Wrangell Narrows, an Inside Passage "shortcut" for small cruise boats and the Alaska State Ferries. (Because it is not a deep water harbour, large cruise ships can't stop there.) The town is located on 547-sq-km (211-sq-mi) Mitkof Island, much of which is national forest and covered by muskeg bog. ■

Left: Houses at low tide at Hammer Slough, Petersburg.
Right: White wildflowers frame Kake harbour.

≈Kake

Kake (pop. 800) is a Tlingit town in "the banana belt" of Southeast, claiming to host the world's tallest (32 m/132.5 ft) totem pole made from a single piece of wood. Historically a dominant nation, the Kake people were known to paddle to northwest Washington in the 1850s where they picked hops for wages at Port Townsend; history reports that Kake Natives killed a customs officer there in 1857. Accounts differ, but subsequent retaliatory actions on the part of the US navy resulted in the destruction of the Kake settlement in 1869. Resettlement eventually followed, but with a Christian influence, resulting in the Kake people's renunciation of Indian ways and the destruction of traditional cultural icons like totem poles and dance regalia. Today cultural traditions are being revived and Native language is taught in local schools. ■

Left: A Kake resident dries black seaweed, laak'ask, a valuable food source for Southeast Native people for thousands of years. More than 80 percent of Southeast's rural households engage in subsistence food gathering, including fish, deer, clams, crab, and berries.

Right: Wrangell Narrows, a narrow, shallow channel between Mitkof and Kupreanof islands, is a 22-mile long byway favoured by Alaska State Ferries, pleasure boats, small cruise ships and other commercial vessels. With over 60 lights and buoys, it is one of the more intimidating navigational challenges on the Inside Passage. This is one of the last markers before entering Petersburg Harbour.

Opposite: White-sided Pacific dolphins play in Chatham Strait.

Chatham Strait and the ABC Islands

Reaching from the Gulf of Alaska 138 nautical miles to Icy Strait, Chatham Strait is the largest of Southeast's inside passages. In places it reaches depths of over 610 m (2000 ft); its widest point is at the southern entrance, about 18 nautical miles between the tip of Baranof Island and Coronation Island, meeting Frederick Sound about one-third of the way north of this entrance. Its southern portion borders Baranof Island on the west and Kuiu Island on the east. The northern part is bounded by Chigagof island on the west and Admiralty island on the east.

These three islands, Admiralty, Baranof and Chichagof, are known as the ABC islands, due to their geographic proximity. The landscape ranges from 1524-m (5000-ft) craggy mountain peaks with spectacular icefields on the west to lower-elevation, gentler landscapes on the east.

The ABC islands support the largest population of brown (grizzly) bears in the world. Admiralty has the largest number with its 4306 sq km (1662 sq mi) home to about 1660 grizzlies, a density of about one per square mile. This species is genetically different from any other bear in the world, related more closely to polar bears than other varieties. Scientists believe that the ancestors of the unique ABC-island bears crossed over from Asia thousands of years ago.

Sitka, one of the oldest cities in the state and the capitol until 1900, is located on the west coast of Baranof Island. Although not on the Inside Passage, it is often visited by cruise ships.

The ABC islands also hold several rainfall records, among them the record for average rainfall, held by Little Port Walter, at the southern end of Baranof Island (559 cm/220 in), and the most rainfall in one day, held by Angoon on Admiralty Island (38.6 cm/15.2 in). ■

Kushtacah

Tales of mysterious human-like creatures exist in cultures all over the world. "Big foot" and "Sasquatch" are two of their common names in North America. Along the Inside Passage, many Sasquatch sightings are in northwestern Washington and the Lower Mainland and central coast of British Columbia.

Although the scientific jury is still out as to whether these creatures actually exist, those who claim to have seen them say Sasquatch are two to three metres tall, covered in hair, ape-like, and generally more curious than aggressive.

Alaska, too, has legends and tales of strange, scientifically unverified, human-like creatures that exist in remote mountainous areas. In Southeast, they call them the Kushtacah, and while similar to Sasquatch, they are not as large and are far more aggressive.

In 1953, local trapper and miner Harry Colp self-published The Strangest Story Ever Told, relating his experiences with the "Kushtacah" in the early part of the twentieth century.

He claims that he was batching with three other prospectors in Wrangell in the spring of 1900 when they heard about a rich source of gold quartz near Thomas Bay, northeast of Petersburg across Frederick Sound. They pooled their resources and sent off one of the men, "Charlie", to look for the shores of a half-moon lake littered with gold nuggets. The other three stayed behind to raise a new grubstake. Charlie returned from his search and quickly boarded the first boat back to the Lower 48.

He had found the half-moon lake and the gold quartz, but just as he was about to make his way back down the mountain he had a horrifying experience. "I hope to God I never see or go through the likes of it again," Colp reports his friend as saying. He described a swarm of terrifying "devils" scrambling up the ridge towards him from the lake. Covered in long coarse hair and scabby running sores, smelling outrageously vile, they tried to grab him, grasping and howling as they swarmed towards him. Charlie left and never returned to Alaska, advising his pals to forget the whole thing.

Not really believing Charlie's story, each of the remaining three men decided to find the lake and see for themselves. And each one had his own nightmare to relate. Scientists have not been able to verify the existence of the Kushtacah or "water devil", but Colp's story is a classic in Southeast.

Harry D. Colp's The Strangest Story Ever Told is sold at local bookstores (Pilot Publishing, Inc. Petersburg, AK 99833).

Hot Springs

One of the great pleasures of past and present travelers along the Inside Passage are the many undeveloped hot springs hiding in out-of-the-way places.

Generally found in regions of young volcanic activity (as with geysers and fumaroles), hot springs occur when surface water finds its way underground through rock fractures and is heated by hotter rock closer to the earth's core. The temperature of the water increases approximately one degree centigrade for every 33 m (108 ft) it descends. The deeper it goes, the hotter it gets. At 2.5 km (1.5 mi) beneath the earth's surface, the temperature is hot enough to boil water. Ground water that reaches this depth percolates back to the earth's surface via other crack systems. The heat of the water and how fast it flows depends on how fast it circulates in the underground channels, how hot it got at its deepest point, and the temperature of the surface water it meets on the way up. As it travels, the water absorbs minerals from the rocks it encounters, minerals which some feel gives it therapeutic properties. The medicinal value is debatable, but hot springs are a wonderful way to ease wary muscles.

Some popular hot springs sites along the Inside Passage include Eucott Bay (near Ocean Falls, BC), Bishop Bay (near Hartley Bay, BC); Tallheo (near Bella Coola, BC); Baranof and Tenakee (off Chatham Strait, AK).

Above: *The "au naturel" hot springs in the mountains above Warm Springs Bay look over a rushing creek emptying into the bay 100 m below.*

Icy Strait

No doubt named for the icebergs that frequently drift along this passage of water, Icy Strait flows about 43 nautical miles from the Inian Islands and Cross Sound on the Gulf of Alaska to Chatham Strait in the east. With many mainland peninsulas and inlets to the north — the most famous of which is Glacier Bay — this weather-prone waterway is bordered by Chichagof Island on the south. An excellent place for whale watching and wildlife viewing, (its average width is 10.5 km/6.5 mi.), Icy Strait is also home to the communities of Hoonah (actually on Port Frederick), Elfin Cove (on Cross Sound) and Gustavus. Treeline in this part of Southeast is about 550 m (1800 ft), compared with 915 m (3000 ft) further south. ■

Opposite left: Tenakee Springs houses overlook Tenakee Arm. The tiny town has a general store, chamber music concerts, and a community bath house in the centre of town fed by a natural hot springs.
Opposite right: A refuge for Soapy Smith's gang when they got kicked out of Skagway in 1898, today the town is a picturesque summer refuge for Juneau residents and passing boaters.
Above: Mt. Fairweather, seen looking west from Icy Strait, is the highest peak in the Fairweather Range, the tallest coastal range on earth.

≈Hoonah

A small Tlingit town of about 800, Hoonah sits on the northern end of Chichagof Island, just off Icy Strait on Port Frederick. According to Tlingit legend, ancestors moved here from Glacier Bay during the last ice age naming it "the place where the north wind doesn't blow". Traditionally villagers have made their living from fur trading, fishing and later logging. As resource-based economies falter, residents are challenged to find new methods of support. ■

SE Alaska's Largest Inside Passage Islands

Island	Square miles	Largest town
Prince of Wales	2,731	Craig
Chicagof	2,062	Hoonah
Admiralty	1,709	Angoon
Baranof	1,636	Sitka
Revillagigedo	1,134	Ketchikan
Kupreanof	1,084	Kake

Jeff Devivi
Hoonah, Alaska

Born in Cordova on the Gulf of Alaska, Jeff Devivi went south to fish, became homesick, hitchhiked a ride north from Bellingham WA, on a seiner, "walked off in Hoonah with a pack on my back and never left". Now a cook at a local restaurant, he helps his partner, Ralphinia, a sheriff's deputy, raise her four children. "It's a great place to raise kids," Devivi says. "The community is small enough that everyone keeps an eye on them. They don't have one father, they have five. But bad apples don't last here; they literally get run out of town. There's no crime rate here at all."

Devivi has been in Hoonah eight years now and has continued fishing, but decided "to take a year off to be a dad to the kids." Like many people who live in small communities on the Inside Passage, Devivi finds it a struggle to make ends meet. "It's tough in the winter," he says. "But if you have a little common sense, you're okay. I trap and fish and hunt. Everything I love is right here in my back yard."

Right: Jeff Devivi in Hoonah, Alaska

≈Glacier Bay
National Park

Ice has been a fixture of Glacier Bay for the last seven million years. About 20,000 years ago, during the height of the most recent great ice age, it would have been possible to walk all the way from here to Cape Cod entirely on ice.

Historians believe that Tlingit people had lived here for thousands of years, until they were chased out by advancing glaciers during the Little Ice Age (which began about 4000 years ago). Some evidences suggests that Tlingit lived in the lower bay area until about 300 years ago, when a final glacial surge made theses lands uninhabitable.

Just 200 years ago, Glacier Bay was totally covered by glacier ice. When Russian explorer Alexis Chirikov (the first non-Native to see the peaks of the Mount Fairweather Range) arrived in 1741, he could not enter Glacier Bay, because it was still a vast ice sheet. George Vancouver visited in 1794, and the bay was just a dent in the shoreline. But by 1879, when naturalist John Muir explored the area, glacial ice had retreated 77 km (48 miles) — a rapid rate of retreat rarely recorded in the world.

Today there are over 200 separate, smaller glaciers in Glacier Bay National Park, 16 of them active tidewater glaciers. It is part of the 24-million-acre Wrangell-St. Elias National Park and Kluane National Park (Canada) World Heritage Site, the world's largest internationally protected area.

Introduced to the world by the writings of Muir and journalist Eliza Scidmore, Glacier Bay was world famous by 1886, attracting boatloads of tourists. Named a national monument

Opposite: Humpback whales often engage in cooperative bubble feeding. They blow bubbles under the water confusing the fish, then surge up through the middle, mouths wide open.
Above: *Sawyer Glacier in Tracy Arm off Stephens Passage. Glaciers store about 75 percent of the world's freshwater.*

in 1925 and a national park in 1980, in 2001 Glacier Bay had over 359,000 visitors, making it one of the most popular tourist destinations in North America. It was named a World Heritage Site in 1992.

People come to see the spectacular glaciers and abundant wildlife, but also to view first-hand the process of post-glacial recolonization by both plants and animals. This process is in various stages throughout the park — ecosystems that range from the bare, seemingly lifeless, rock recently covered by glaciers to thick, lush forest lands. Scientific research covers everything from glacial dynamics and underwater habitats to acoustic monitoring of marine mammals and fish distribution.

Today marine mammals in the park area include cetaceans (humpback, killer and gray whales; harbour and Dall's porpoises), seals and sea lions, 30 to 40 species of land mammals and 240 species of birds. Scientists also estimate 200 species of fish live in these waters. ■

Above left: *Spectators are dwarfed by an arching iceberg in Tracy Arm. Nine-tenths of an iceberg's surface is underwater.*

Above right: *Aurora borealis, seen here over Juneau, is a phenomenon caused when sun spot activity releases charged atoms into space. When some of these particles fall towards earth, they are pulled towards the north and south poles by the earth's magnetic field. The ensuing light displays are most commonly seen in the northern latitudes in spring and fall and on very clear nights during the winter. The lowest Aurora are about 64 km (40 mi) from earth's surface, but they can extend 965 km (600 mi) into the atmosphere. In Tlingit tradition the appearance of "the northern lights" is a sign of impending battle.*

Stephens Passage

Although 88-nautical-mile-long Stephens Passage is a major north-south route, it's quite possible to find yourself alone on this stretch of water. Juneau carpenter Dean Blust tells of a friend who was kayaking across it one day. "She was by herself," says Blust, "and she was feeling real nervous and alone and too far from shore. All of a sudden, this whale came up next to her. It didn't even sound. It just came up next to her and then swam on the surface right beside her. It did this for about four miles. Right next to her. Eye to eye. Until she was close to shore."

Connecting Frederick Sound in the south with Lynn Canal in the north, it is a common place to see whales. It is bounded by Admiralty Island on the west and the ice covered peaks of the Coast Range on the east, making icebergs from Tracy and Endicott arms another common sight. Many claim that Smith Sawyer Glacier at Tracy Arm provides the most spectacular glacier-viewing in Southeast. Glaciers can also be viewed close-hand up Taku Inlet in Hobart Bay. ■

"But at length the clouds lifted a little, and beneath their gray fringes I saw the berg-filled expanse of the bay, and the feet of the mountains that stand about it, and the imposing fronts of five huge glaciers, the nearest being immediately beneath me. This was my first general view of Glacier Bay, a solitude of ice and snow and newborn rocks, dim, dreary, mysterious."

John Muir. Travels in Alaska (1879)

Glaciers

Glaciers, which cover one-tenth of the earth's surface, form when more snow falls than melts. At higher elevations the snow piles up and compresses into large thick ice masses (ablation); at lower elevations it melts. Over time, the ice compresses sufficiently so that any air pockets become very tiny. When glacier ice becomes extremely dense, the ice absorbs all other colors in the spectrum and reflects primarily blue, which is what we see. White glacier ice indicates the presence of many tiny air bubbles still in the ice.

What makes glaciers unique is their ability to move. When the compressed ice reaches a critical thickness, about 18 m (59 ft), the weight forces movement. A glacier can grow to be over 100 km (62 mi) long or as small as a football field.

Retreating glaciers provide many fascinating opportunities for study, particularly as vegetation is introduced and begins to grow. Algae, lichens and moss come first, stabilizing silts and providing "anchors" on rock, followed by more complex organisms like horsetail, dryas, and eventually mature forests.

There are several types of glaciers: ice sheets, ice caps, ice streams, outlet glaciers, ice fields, mountain glaciers, valley glaciers, piedmont glaciers, cirque glaciers, hanging glaciers, and tidewater glaciers.

On the Inside Passage, tidewater glaciers, with their calving icebergs, provide the most spectacular viewing. As the name implies, these are valley glaciers that flow far enough to reach out into the sea. There are nine tidewater glaciers in Glacier Bay.

Top: Tidewater glaciers come right to the water's edge, "calving" icebergs into the ocean.
Bottom: Margerie Glacier at the head of Tarr Inlet in Glacier Bay is about 1.5 km (0.9 mi) wide and 22 km (14 mi) long.

John Muir

"To sit in solitude, to think in solitude with only the music of the stream and the cedar to break the glow of silence, here lies the value of wilderness." - John Muir

John Muir was perhaps America's most famous naturalist and conservationist. His writings helped to establish and preserve Glacier Bay as a national park. One of the founders of the Sierra Club, he has, in fact, been called the father of America's national parks, also influencing the creation of Yosemite, Sequoia, Mount Rainier and Grand Canyon national parks.

Born in Scotland in 1838, Muir's family moved to Wisconsin when he was 11. He grew up on a farm there, developing a great love of nature and attracting attention with his inventions, including clocks that kept accurate time and a wondrous device that tipped him out of bed before dawn. Even though he had no formal education, he entered the University of Wisconsin at the age of 22, where he studied for two years. He arrived in California in 1868, beginning a life-long love affair with Yosemite.

Based on his observations there, he championed an 1840 theory of continental glaciation that changed scientific thought. In 1879, he travelled to Alaska to study active glaciers. Accompanied by Tlingit Indian guides and his missionary friend S. Hall Young, and using Capt. George Vancouver's charts, he became the first to chart and explore Glacier Bay. At that time, the ice had only recently receded, opening the bay to navigation. Braving the onset of winter weather, he mapped the area for the U.S. Government, who named the main tidewater glacier after him.

Altogether he made seven trips to Alaska, writing of his explorations and discoveries extensively. By his 1890 trip to Glacier Bay, he was rubbing elbows with tourist excursion boats.

During his lifetime he published 300 articles and 10 major books, among them Travels in Alaska and the

Above: *John Muir and Theodore Roosevelt in Yosemite, CA, c 1906*
Top: *Fish boat in Glacier Bay*

classic Stickeen, a true story of a dramatic struggle that Muir and a dog shared on an Alaskan glacier. "Our storm-battle for life brought him to light," wrote Muir of the dog, "and through him as through a window I have ever since been looking with deeper sympathy into all my fellow mortals."

Dedicated to conservation, Muir influenced contemporaries like Ralph Waldo Emerson and US President Theodore Roosevelt. He died on Christmas Eve 1914, leaving behind an invaluable legacy.

Dean Blust,
Carpenter
and Chris Blust,
Administrator, Juneau

A lot of people who live in Alaska have come from someplace else, Chris and Dean Blust of Juneau among them. While there are probably as many reasons for moving north as there are people who do so, for the Blusts, it was simple. "The main reason was to have a safe place to raise our daughter," says Chris. "And it was."

But the Blusts' daughter is an adult now, and they stay on. "It's a place where you're really close to nature," says Chris. They live about a mile from Mendenhall Glacier and routinely see wildlife that ranges from bear to salmon and beaver.

"Everything here keeps you really connected," the former Washingtonian says, "people, nature, the ocean." They own kayaks and a 26-foot powerboat and spend as much time as possible on the water, despite weather that isn't always cooperative. "If you live in Southeast Alaska, you have to go rain or shine, or you don't go anywhere," she says.

Chris admits that the lack of light in winter is a little wearing. Fortunately her employer, like many in Juneau, offers two weeks of paid vacation mid-winter for the express purpose of heading south. The light isn't a problem for Dean. He enjoys what he describes as "all the palettes of grey." And in Juneau there's a lot of grey — on the shortest day of the year, the area receives only about six hours of sunlight. Year round, only one out of every 10 days is clear. "But I haven't had a single day since we moved here that I felt like we shouldn't have," he says. "I just like being surrounded by the mountains and the ocean."

To Dean, one of the biggest plusses of living in Alaska is the

Above: *Dean and Christ Blust at Mendenhall Glacier*

freedom and the responsibility that comes with that. "Out on the water," he says, "if you do something stupid, you're going to have to deal with it. The illusion of protection that a lot of people have down south is just that — an illusion."

He recalls one kayak trip with a friend when the weather changed unexpectedly while they were crossing Icy Strait just outside Glacier Bay. "The wind came up and the fog came in and we couldn't see land," he recalls (When they got into shore they learned the wind speed was 55 knots).

"The wind was going against a 20-foot tide and it was pretty terrifying," he admits. "But we kept paddling. It was all you could do." "Every wave was breaking over my head and some of them would break so hard that you'd open your eyes and there was nothing but green around." A trip that was supposed to take 45 minutes stretched into four hours. "You just think, 'Okay, make it over this one,'" Dean recalls. He remembers getting picked up by a water spout that lifted him about seven feet in the air. "I'm not trying

to make it sound heroic," he says, "because it wasn't. It was just one of those experiences that when you got to the other side, you were different."

On another occasion Dean was kayaking with another friend in Glacier Bay when a whale breached right beside them. "Its flukes were hanging up in the air right over my friend's boat and dripping down on her. And in the time it took me to think, 'Well, it's going to break her boat, and I'm going to have to get her ashore,' the whale just came down and turned 90 degrees and slid down into the water. She said it was just an inch away from her boat the whole time. It could have hit us if it wanted to."

"The main thing I got thinking about afterwards," Dean recalls, "was that I'm out there in a state-of-the-art ocean kayak and everything out there is better at it than I am. You're looking around, and you're paddling, and there's nobody around, and it doesn't matter if you live or die. And I like it. It really puts things in perspective."

Above: Decker Brothers Building in downtown Juneau, 1893.

≈Juneau

Although Juneau (pop. 29,000) is Alaska's state capitol, it is named after a Canadian — Quebec-born miner Joe Juneau. Along with his partner Richard Harris, Juneau discovered pebble-sized gold nuggets on Gold Creek, which runs through present day Juneau, in 1880, (with a lot of help from Chief Kowee, an Auk Indian who lived on Admiralty Island, and George Pilz, a Sitka entrepreneur). Within a year, 300 miners had moved in. To some disagreement, Harris named the settlement after himself, but when local miners voted, Harrisburg was out and Juneau was in. (Some accounts suggest Juneau bought the votes with his earnings.) The strike turned out to be one of the largest lodes of gold quartz in the world. Today, its Victorian homes, mountain-hugging steep wooden staircases, and historic storefronts evoke the early days when mining was king.

Juneau is located on the Gastineau Channel and is surrounded by tall mountains: Mt. Juneau (1090m/3576 ft) on one side and Mt. Roberts (1116 m/3819 ft) on the other. To the east is the Juneau Icefield, where receding tidewater Mendenhall Glacier lies, Southeast's most accessible.

Although it is on the mainland, Juneau is not connected by road to the "outside", making it the only state capitol in the US so blessed — although discussion of such a road is often on the agenda. Assuming the role as centre of state government in 1900, today about half of Juneau's economy comes from that function. A stop on all Inside Passage cruise-boat routes, Juneau is further bolstered by tourism. ∎

Lynn Canal

On a beautiful day the scenery along Lynn Canal is unmatchable on the Inside Passage. Towering on one side are the Kakuhan and Chilkoot ranges of the Coast Mountains and on the other, the Chilkat Range and the Takhinsha mountains. Glaciers, (like Davidson and Rainbow glaciers south of Haines), snowfields, and bare craggy rock peaks provide endless opportunities to observe glaciation and its effects.

Lynn Canal stretches 83 nautical miles from its intersection with Icy Strait in the south to historic Skagway in the north and it's easy to put yourself back to 1897 and 1898 when thousands of men, women and children travelled on ships from southern ports like Seattle, Vancouver and San Francisco with little backing them but the dream of gold.

Fishermen call it "the Big Lynn." On a benign day, this seems like a pleasant stretch of water, but the conditions here can change on a whim, particularly if the wind opposes the tide. The high mountains create a funnel for winds, which in the winter, can reach up to 70 knots. Several high profile shipwrecks have taken place here, the *Clara Nevada* (1898), the *Princess May* (1910) and the *Princess Kathleen* (1952) among them. Some, like the *Princess Sophia*, had tragic consequences. Remembered as the worst maritime disaster in the history of Pacific northwest shipping, this CPR passenger vessel was holed when it struck Vanderbilt Reef in 1918 during a blizzard, resulting in the loss of all 343 passengers and crew.

The two major settlements on Lynn Canal are Haines, at the head of Chilkoot Inlet, and historic Skagway, at the head of Taiya Inlet, and the end of the Inside Passage. ■

Above: *Eldred Rock Light Station in Lynn Canal is the oldest remaining lighthouse in Alaska. No longer manned, it began operation in June 1906. The* SS Clara Nevada *sank here in 1898, with a loss of 100 lives, securing a place for itself in local legend when it resurfaced some ten years later. The light station's hexagonal shape reflects the influence of early Russian settlers.*

Above: History has a long list of vessels that have run aground in Lynn Canal. The CPR's SS Princess May *found herself high and dry on Sentinel Island, north of Juneau, in 1910. All 168 passengers and crew were safely rescued, but the vessel was stuck on the reef for a month before she could be towed off, repaired and returned to service.*

≈Haines

An unassuming town, Haines (pop. 2500) may be among the most beautifully situated in the world. Dramatically back-dropped by the 1981-m (6500-ft) Cathedral Peaks, it was originally named Dei Shu, which means "end of the trail". Missionaries renamed the town after a Presbyterian Church member, who, sadly for her, never visited.

Like most towns of the Inside Passage Haines' economy is based on commercial fishing and mining, although tourism is also important. One of only three towns in Southeast that is connected to the outside world by highway, visitors are often reminded that Haines is only 20 km (13 mi) by water from Skagway, but 578 km (359 mi) by road. The town is also a stop on the Alaska State Ferries' route.

Despite being on the road to somewhere and therefore fairly accessible, Haines has a low-key charm. There are no glitzy gift and souvenir stores. Several shops offer unique items made by local artists.

The main attraction, Fort Seward National Historic Monument, was built between 1902 and 1904 to establish an American military presence when the US-Canada border was in dispute. It was the first permanent — and until WWII, the only — army post in Alaska, and because of its remote location was often considered a foreign posting. Another major attraction is the 48,000-acre Alaska Chilkat Bald Eagle Preserve. Allegedly the largest concentration of American bald eagles in the world (three to four thousand of them) come to feast on the late Chilkat River salmon run October through December. ■

Above left: *The Cathedral Peaks of the Chilkat Range give Haines a spectacular setting.*
Above right: *Detail of totem pole, Haines.*
Left: *Officers and crew from around the world have left their mark on the steep rock wall at Skagway's cruise ship dock.*

≈Skagway

Skagway is the tiny town with the huge history that is the northern terminus of the Inside Passage. It is also a terminus for the historic White Pass and Yukon Railway (now an excursion line), the Alaska Marine Highway System, and a branch of the now abandoned Canol (Canadian Oil) pipeline.

The town sprang up almost overnight in 1897 as a result of the rush to the Klondike goldfields. Today it enjoys a different kind of boom as hundreds of thousands of tourists visit each year, most of them on cruise ships and the Alaska State Ferries, some by road. Although early residents had to trek over Chilkoot or White passes to get to the outside world, today Skagway is connected by highway to Whitehorse, Yukon Territory. The Chilkoot Trail, part of the Klondike Gold Rush International Historic Park, is used by hikers and historians.

In its heyday, Skagway had a population of about 20,000. Today its fulltime residents number about 700, although in the summertime that raises to about 2500.

At the same latitude as Stockholm, Sweden, it enjoys a relatively dry climate with an average of only 66 cm (26 in) of rain (and 99 cm/39 in of snow) annually. Besides tourism, Skagway's economy also relies on shipping. ■

Above: Once Klondikers completed the Inside Passage leg of their journey, they had only begun. These hopefuls are on the shore at Dyea, near Skagway, each with a ton of supplies.

Opposite: A boatload of gold-fevered citizens arrives in Skagway in 1898.

Klondike Gold Rush

News of the rich 1896 gold strike on a tributary of the Klondike River in the Yukon valley reached the world when the SS *Excelsior* docked in San Francisco and the SS *Portland* docked in Seattle in July 1897. The scruffy miners disembarking from both vessels carried both the gold they had mined and hope for thousands of people hit hard by a world-wide depression. Soon there was a stampede north of men, women and even a few children.

Getting to the goldfields was enormously difficult. Once the stampede began, regular steamships were quickly booked, which meant desperate miners willingly paid for passage on unseaworthy vessels. If they arrived in Skagway or Dyea and managed to get their goods ashore (the RCMP in Canada wouldn't allow miners into the Klondike without at least a years' worth of supplies), the Klondikers still had to get themselves and their ton of goods to the Yukon via one of the horrific mountain passes.

The Chilkoot and White Pass trails were ancient Native routes that took miners from the head of Lynn Canal through the mountains over the Yukon River system to Dawson City. Those who could afford it hired Indian packers and/or horses to carry their supplies. Those who couldn't, packed the stuff on their backs, making 20 or 30 gruelling trips over several months.

Avalanches, bitter cold, slippery mud and precipitous rocky ledges were only part of the difficulties. The Klondike Gold Rush also attracted unscrupulous opportunists who took advantage of the naivete and desperation of the miners. The infamous Soapy Smith and his gang of 300 ne'er-do-wells left a bloody legacy of swindle, rape, murder, and robbery along the Chilkoot Trail. (The White Pass and Yukon Railway finally opened for business in 1899, but just as the rush was fading.)

Within six months in 1897, an estimated 100,000 hopeful souls set out for the goldfields. Thousands, facing starvation, violence, and exhaustion died along the way or turned back. Only about three out of every ten who started actually made it to the Klondike.

Dawson City became the headquarters of the gold rush, an instant city built at the confluence of the Yukon and Klondike rivers, with a population of over 40,000 at its height. Known as the Paris of the North, it offered caviar and champagne to those who could afford it, exhaustion, disillusionment, and despair for those less lucky.

The Klondike Kings, a handful of miners who got in on the strike early, took over one billion dollars of gold out of the ground by current values. However, most arriving in 1898 found that all of the claims had been staked and their survival of unbearable hardships had been for naught.

Broadway in Skagway as it looked in 1897 (inset) and 1899 (main).

Left: *Travel on the Chilkoot Trail was not limited to men. These actresses were among tens of thousands bound for the Klondike in 1897.*

Right: *A party of miners with their makeshift ladder scales a snow-covered portion of the Dyea Trail.*

Opposite top: *The "Golden Stair" over the Chilkoot Pass had 1500 steps cut into the ice at a 45-degree angle, covering the last 610 m (2000 ft) of elevation in 16 km (10 mi). The whole trail was 48 km (30 mi) long, climbing 1067 m (3500 ft). This photo was taken in the spring of 1898.*

Opposite bottom: *Soapy at the bar of his Skagway Saloon in 1898. Soapy Smith and his gang allegedly ran Skagway using a variety of illegal and violent tactics until Smith was gunned down in 1898. A con man from a once-wealthy Georgia family, Jefferson Randolph Smith earned his nickname in the legendary Colorado town of Leadville when he ran a soap-selling scam.*

Some turned around and went home. Others opened businesses or offered themselves as day labourers. (Fred Trump, Donald Trump's grandfather, allegedly earned a fortune running the Arctic Restaurant and Hotel in Bennett, BC, along the Chilkoot Trail.)

Although the actual rush lasted only two years, it has captured the imagination of the world for over a century. Jack London, Robert Service, Pierre Berton and James Michener are among those whose writings have kept the stories and legends alive. ■

Index

Photographic Credits

All photographs by Ron Woodward except on the following pages:

Alaska State Library: 105 bottom left (PCA 20-142), 132 (PCA 344-57), 140 right (PCA 20-48), 141 bottom (ASL 277-1-9)

British Columbia Archives: 9 (na-39711), 17 (a-03227), 19 (d-00417), 21 bottom (i-28888), 22 top (f-09327), 24 top (a-07086), 24 bottom (i-33614), 27 top (i-51777), 36 (a-00903), 38 top (b-03620), 38 bottom (e-03113), 44-5 (b-06377), 47 (a-00009), 48 left (e-06689), 48 right (e-00521), 55 (d-08490), 56 (d-02330), 61 (h-07091), 65 (h-03982), 68 (d-08473), 70 (h-01122), 73 (a-09131), 76-77 (h-06508), 79 (i-33619), 82 top (i-50641), 84 (b-03570), 83 top left (pdp 02244), 98 (g-04699), 99 (b-03574), 104 (c-08954), 106-7 (d-08356), 116 (d-02228), 136 (g-02070), 137 (i-51625)

Canadian National Archives: 15

City of Vancouver Archives: 46 (a04601)

Brian Falconer: 5, 12 left & right, 13 left & right, 27 bottom right, 39 right, 75 left, 85 bottom, 103 bottom, 110 bottom, 112 top left, 118 bottom, 126 top, 127, 128 left, 129 top & bottom

Michael Hayward: 92-3

Library of Congress: 2, 130

Nancy Little: 51 left

Ian McAllister: 90, 95

US National Oceanic and Atmospheric Administration: 128 right

Walter and Marvis Norman: 91 top right

Esther Schmidt: 60, 119

Sharksong/M. Kazmers: 57

University of Washington Archives: 7 (La Roche 10022), 14 (NA 2567), 20-21 (NA 3792), 105 top (NA 2094), 105 bottom right (NA 2103), 134 (Cobb 3138), 138 inset (La Roche 372), 138-139 (La Roche 407), 140 left (La Roche 2049), 141 top (UW 13669)

Vancouver Public Library: 25 (VPL 1677)

John Walls: 35

Allison Watt: 27 bottom left

Amber Woodward: 144 main

Meredith Bain Woodward: 88 top right, 93 bottom, 120 right, 123, 124 bottom

About the Authors

Along with their second mate, Salsa, Ron and Meredith Woodward have been sailing the Pacific Northwest for 15 years, currently on a 40-foot 1975 Valiant, the *Erramus*. He is a photographer, graphic designer and senior lecturer in the graduate publishing program at Simon Fraser University in Vancouver. She is an award-winning writer, editor and actor. Salsa is a dog. They have written two other books for Altitude: *British Columbia Interior: An Altitude SuperGuide* and *Land of Dreams: A History in Photographs of the British Columbia Interior.*

Right: The authors aboard the Erramus, *with* second mate Salsa *(inset).*